Strategies for Common Core Mathematics

Implementing the Standards for Mathematical Practice, 6–8

Leslie A. Texas and Tammy L. Jones

Eye On Education
6 Depot Way West, Suite 106
Larchmont, NY 10538
(914) 833-0551
(914) 833-0761 fax
www.eyeoneducation.com

Library of Congress Cataloging-in-Publication Data

Texas, Leslie A.
Strategies for common core mathematics. Implementing the standards for mathematical
practice, 6–8/Leslie A. Texas and Tammy L. Jones.
       pages   cm
ISBN 978-1-59667-243-7
1. Mathematics—Study and teaching (Middle school)
2. Mathematics—Study and teaching (Middle school)—Standards—United States.
I. Jones, Tammy L.
II. Title.
QA135.6.J6625 2013
510.71′273—dc23   2013001370

10 9 8 7 6 5 4 3 2 1

Sponsoring Editor: Robert Sickles
Production Editor: Lauren Beebe
Copyeditor: Laurie Lieb
Designer and Compositor: Matthew Williams, click! Publishing Services
Cover Designer: Armen Kojoyian

Also Available from Eye On Education

Acknowledgments

We would first like to thank Eye On Education for the opportunity to develop this series of books. A special thank you to Bob Sickles, President of Eye On Education, for his continued support and patience throughout this project. To the editorial staff, thank you for your excellent guidance and expeditious feedback. We would also like to express gratitude to the many students, teachers, schools, and districts with which we have worked over the years. You have allowed us the opportunity to develop, use, and refine these strategies in classrooms across the country. Finally, thanks to our families for their support and encouragement while on this journey.

Meet the Authors

Leslie A. Texas has over twenty years of experience working with K–12 teachers and schools across the country to enhance rigorous and relevant instruction. She believes that improving student outcomes depends on comprehensive approaches to teaching and learning. She taught middle- and high-school mathematics and science, and has strong content expertise in both areas. Through her advanced degree studies, she honed her skills in content and program development and student-centered instruction. Using a combination of direct instruction, modeling, and problem-solving activities rooted in practical application of mathematical principles, Leslie helps teachers become more effective classroom leaders and peer coaches.

An educator since 1979, **Tammy L. Jones** has worked with students from first grade through college. Currently, Tammy is consulting with individual school districts in training mathematics teachers on effective techniques for being successful in the mathematics classroom. As a classroom teacher Tammy's goal was that all students understand and appreciate the mathematics they were studying; that they could read it, write it, explore it, and communicate it with confidence; and that they would be able to use mathematics as they need to in their lives. She believes that problem solving, followed by a well-reasoned presentation of results, is central to the process of learning mathematics, and that this learning happens most effectively in a cooperative, student-centered classroom. Tammy believes that mathematics is experiential and in her current consulting work creates and shares mathematical experiences.

A lifelong learner, Tammy is an active member in the National Council of Teachers of Mathematics and its Tennessee affiliates as well as a T^3 Instructor for Texas Instruments. Serving on the Mathematics Feedback Group for the Common Core Standards gave Tammy a unique perspective on the development of the Standards and allowed special insight into the development of this series.

Supplemental Downloads

Several of the figures discussed and displayed in this book are also available on Eye On Education's website as Adobe Acrobat files. Permission has been granted to purchasers of this book to download these resources and print them.

You can access the downloads by visiting www.eyeoneducation.com. From the home page, click on the "Free" tab, and then click on "Supplemental Downloads." Alternatively, you can search or browse our website for this book's product page, and click on "Log in to Access Supplemental Downloads."

Your book-buyer access code is **SCC-7243-7**.

Index of Supplemental Downloads

Contents

Foreword

Will Rogers is credited with saying, "When you are dissatisfied and unhappy with your adult life and think you would like to return to your youth, you will feel better if you remember you would have to take Algebra." Although said in jest, many adults remember the frustrations and lack of success they experienced in mathematics. In spite of increased efforts to improve the teaching of mathematics in the past two decades, Algebra I remains one of the highest failing courses in U.S. schools. For current students, the rigor proposed in the Common Core mathematics standards adds to their fears and frustrations. Teachers and school administrators will find the three books written by Leslie A. Texas and Tammy L. Jones helpful in preparing students, beginning in kindergarten, to think mathematically and come to enjoy participating in such thinking. In a unique way, these talented authors provide:

- ◆ Strategies for engaging students in mathematical discussions
- ◆ Strategies that allow for differentiation—both individually and in small groups
- ◆ Strategies that involve cooperative learning environments and small-group problem solving
- ◆ Strategies that can be tools for diagnosing student misconceptions and then making modifications for individual student needs; for example, some of the books' Guided Facilitation sections identify common student misconceptions and ideas for addressing them
- ◆ Questioning strategies that allow students to arrive at the "ah-ha" moment when investigating a topic so they can create their own understanding upon which later topics will be built. This practice is a critical shift in what traditionally has been the delivery of mathematics instruction. This concept of teaching is critical throughout the grade levels if we ever expect to address the high failure rates in Algebra I.

Collectively, Texas and Jones have 40 years of classroom experience teaching mathematics in elementary, middle, and high schools, which include teaching in urban, suburban, rural, and private school settings. Being active members of their professional organizations, such as the National Council of Teachers of Mathematics (NCTM), has allowed them to model lifelong learning for both their students and their peers.

In addition to their classroom teaching, these skilled authors have provided professional development for teachers and students from kindergarten through college level in 40 states. Their work has included helping develop standards and curriculum at the state level as well as implementing curriculum and best-practice strategies at the classroom level. One of the characteristics that places Texas and Jones in heavy demand as consultants is their ability to model and offer teachers support throughout the school year, a practice that builds capacity at both building and district levels. As a result of the authors' consulting experiences, all of the strategies contained in this series have been implemented successfully in multiple classrooms around the country.

Educators who have the responsibility of teaching mathematics will find the strategies provided in these three books to be critical tools in improving the mathematical skills of students in grades K–12. If implemented with fidelity, eventually Will Rogers can be proven wrong by increasing the number of adults who reflect on their youth and think of Algebra as a positive experience! (Or think of Algebra positively!)

Robert Lynn Canady, Professor Emeritus
University of Virginia, Charlottesville, VA

Preface:
A Note to Our Readers

When we took on the task of writing this book, we asked ourselves two questions: So What? and Who Cares? Why write a book about the mathematical practices and how could we do it in such a way that would make a difference? These were certainly the questions that guided our process as we developed the materials contained within these pages. Practical, versatile, easy to implement, promotes student engagement, yields results— these were the criteria we used as a guideline for selecting the strategies for this book. Other questions we thought might be of interest as well as our responses are listed below:

Why are the same strategies used in all three books in the series?

We intentionally chose strategies versatile enough to be used across the grade levels so we could illustrate the progression of concept development designed in the Common Core State Standards for Mathematics. Explicitly illustrating the scaffolding of skills across the levels emphasizes the importance of developing the mathematical practices at each level to ensure success as students transition to the next level.

How can I teach all my content standards using the strategies in this book?

All the strategies contained in this book are versatile and can be used with any content standards you choose. We have included content-specific examples to illustrate how the strategy works, but none of the strategies are limited to the mathematical concepts shown.

How do I know these strategies will work in my classroom?

These are proven strategies that have been implemented in our own classrooms as well as in hundreds of classrooms around the country. They were intentionally chosen based on their ease of use and the impact they have had on student engagement and achievement. Some of the strategies were shared by teachers with whom we work; permission for their use has been given.

How can I develop mathematical thinkers *and* provide an opportunity for computational proficiency?

The Common Core requires that students be able to engage in mathematical discourse using their understanding and knowledge of the mathematical content. In order to gain mastery, they need to practice the skills. This means working math problems in order to become computationally proficient. So how can you take a basic problem set and make it into a rich and engaging task? This book contains specific strategies that illustrate how to engage students in computational practice; other strategies promote higher-order thinking and in-depth problem solving.

Why would I buy this book when there is so much free stuff out there?

There are many fantastic resources available on the Internet. For example, the sites containing assessment tasks addressing the critical content and skills of the Common Core State Standards are tremendously valuable. The value of this book is that it not only contains strategies to prepare students for these rigorous assessments, but also provides practical notes on how to implement them effectively. You can even take the released items from the websites and use them as the content for the strategies shared in the book.

The Doorway to the Common Core

The Common Core State Standards for Mathematics

With the creation of the Common Core State Standards for Mathematics (CCSSM), a new era in mathematics education began for those states that adopted them. States that have adopted the CCSSM now have a common goal in mathematics education.

> Building on the excellent foundation of standards states have laid, the Common Core State Standards are the first step in providing our young people with a high-quality education. It should be clear to every student, parent, and teacher what the standards of success are in every school. (Common Core State Standards Initiative, 2012a)

How clear is it "what the standards of success are"? The standards were written "to provide a clear and consistent framework to prepare our children for college and the workforce" (Common Core State Standards Initiative, 2012a).

In its *Myths vs Facts* section, the CORE Standards website (www .corestandards.org/about-the-standards/myths-vs-facts) states that the standards "are not a curriculum. They are a clear set of shared goals and expectations for what knowledge and skills will help our students succeed." What are the implications for the classroom teacher, whether teaching kindergarten or high-school algebra? Teachers need to become fluent in the content not only to teach their grade and course, but also to reinforce the prior content knowledge of their students and understand how the current content supports where the students are going. Only through studying these progressions will teachers truly be able to connect the mathematics they are teaching to what their students have previously learned and to what will be expected of them in upcoming grades.

The Standards for Mathematical Practice

According to the Common Core State Standards for Mathematics, "The Standards for Mathematical Practice describe varieties of expertise that mathematics educators at all levels should seek to develop in their students" (2012b). The National Council of Teachers of Mathematics (NCTM), in its *Principles and Standards for School Mathematics (PSSM)*, states that "the five Process Standards highlight ways of acquiring and applying content knowledge" (2005, p. 29).

The Standards for Mathematical Practice (SMP) are based upon the NCTM process standards and the strands of mathematical proficiency in the National Research Council's report *Adding It Up*. NCTM chose to present its mathematical processes from the point of view that these are a collection of best practices that teachers can utilize to help their students develop a depth of understanding of key mathematical concepts that also leads to increased retention of those concepts.

Here are the eight Standards for Mathematical Practice (Common Core State Standards Initiative, 2012b):

1. Make sense of problems and persevere in solving them.
2. Reason abstractly and quantitatively.
3. Construct viable arguments and critique the reasoning of others.
4. Model with mathematics.
5. Use appropriate tools strategically.
6. Attend to precision.
7. Look for and make use of structure.
8. Look for and express regularity in repeated reasoning.

The content standards provide the context, whereas the Standards for Mathematical Practice assist students in developing mathematical proficiency. The eight practices are distinct from one another but interconnected in ways that support students in becoming mathematically proficient. Expertise is generated in practice but implemented through process.

Expertise is generated in practice but implemented through process.

These practices need to be incorporated into daily classroom instruction. The creators of the Common Core State Standards for Mathematics took the perspective that the Standards for Mathematical Practice are observable indicators of student understanding that identify the level of expertise that teachers should foster in their students. The writers for the CCSSM even argue that a lack of understanding in the mathematical content inhibits students from participating in the mathematical practices. But it is the practices themselves that help develop that understanding. So connecting the content to the mathematical practices is critical if teachers want to develop solid mathematical proficiency in their students (Common Core State Standards Initiative, 2012b).

Will these mathematical practices look the same in a kindergarten classroom as in a high-school mathematics classroom? Not necessarily. The students are at a different level in their journey toward attaining expertise in various mathematical topics and skills. Students need procedural fluency in a topic as well as an understanding of the concept. **It is for this reason there are three books in this series so these differences can be addressed specifically for each grade band.**

The processes are how a student gains proficiencies in the content that allows them to develop the practices that ultimately carry them through their mathematical journey. The CCSSM are a collection of processes, proficiencies, and practices that produces students who are ready for successful transition into the workplace or college.

The Standards for Mathematical Practice versus the Content Standards

The Standards for Mathematical Practice identify the habits that mathematically proficient students have developed. Habits are developed over time. How long it takes to develop a habit is debatable. But clearly, mathematically proficient students, those who have developed these eight habits, have experienced mathematics regularly and consistently over a period of time.

The Standards for Mathematical Practice are how the student engages with the mathematical content to develop both procedural fluency and conceptual understanding. They are separate, yet must be developed together to ensure that students can effectively understand the content and engage in the practices. The processes are how students gain proficiencies in the content that allow them to develop the practices that ultimately become sound habits.

> The processes are how students gain proficiencies in the content that allow them to develop the practices that ultimately become sound habits.

How the Standards for Mathematical Practice Support the Content Standards

For students to connect the practices to the content, teachers need to understand how students learn mathematics and that not all students learn the same way or in the same time frame. Teachers will need to provide opportunities for students to delve deeply into a concept by designing lessons that explicitly embed and utilize the Standards for Mathematical Practice.

The eight Standards for Mathematical Practice are not experienced in isolation. In fact, most of the time, students simultaneously employ several of the practices as they engage in mathematical experiences. If students are to "construct viable arguments and critique the reasoning of others," they will need to "attend to precision" by using precise vocabulary and symbolism. They will then check the reasonableness of their solutions by gathering supporting evidence. Students who "look for and make use of structure" will also "look for and express regularity in repeated reasoning" while they "make sense of problems and persevere in solving them." Along the way they also "use appropriate tools strategically."

The content standards also support the practices. The writers identify "potential 'points of intersection'" between the content and the SMP as places where the content mastery requires a level of deeper understanding.

The Partnership for Assessment of Readiness for College and Careers (PARCC) Content Framework for Mathematics notes that "opportunities for in-depth work on key concepts and connections to critical practices . . . intend to support . . . efforts to deliver instruction that connects content and practices while achieving the standards' balance of conceptual understanding, procedural skill and fluency, and application" (n.d., para. 3).

Teaching the Standards for Mathematical Practice

Teaching students to become mathematical thinkers does not happen randomly. In order for students to meet the expectations of high-level content knowledge contained in the CCSSM, it is necessary for the students to build a foundation of thinking and communicating mathematically. These practices, outlined in the Standards for Mathematical Practice, must be explicitly and intentionally designed into the curriculum and become a focus of instructional practice in the classroom.

The next section contains strategies for teaching the mathematical practices while simultaneously addressing the content of the Common Core State Standards for Mathematics. These ideas were chosen for their flexibility: they can be taught at any grade level and address almost any concept. In addition, they are easy to prepare and implement. This allows for continued use and refinement while, at the same time, not requiring an added burden of hours of preparation. The section contains an overall description as well as detailed directions for implementation of each strategy. See the Strategies Matrix (page 8) for an overview of the mapping of each strategy to the SMP.

The Doorway to the Standards for Mathematical Practice

The Standards for Mathematical Practice can be seen as the doorway to implementing the Common Core State Standards for Mathematics. Students, as well as educators and administrators, need to understand what these eight practices entail and what they might look like in their classrooms and mathematical experiences. These standards can be grouped into various clusters to represent differing foci. For the purpose of developing strategies to support the implementation of the CCSSM, the SMP can be grouped as shown in the doorway graphic (page 6).

A door provides the first impression of what lies beyond. When the door is open, it invites one to enter and experience what is behind it. When a door is closed, it evokes a sense of mystery and the unknown. For some educators, the SMP are an open door to the CCSSM. These educators are familiar with implementing process standards through research-based strategies and guiding their students to a deeper understanding of mathematical concepts. For others, the SMP are viewed as a locked door through which they have yet to enter. They have guided their students to a library filled with procedural worksheets and surface-skimming algorithmic mathematics.

**Standards for
Mathematical Practice**

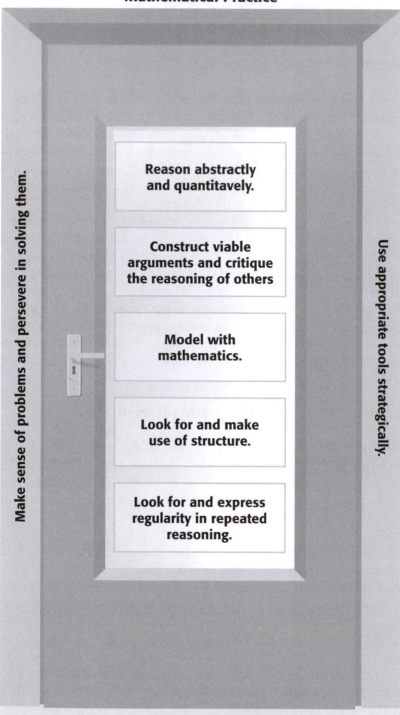

Make sense of problems and persevere in solving them.

Use appropriate tools strategically.

**Reason abstractly
and quantitavely.**

**Construct viable
arguments and critique
the reasoning of others**

**Model with
mathematics.**

**Look for and make
use of structure.**

**Look for and express
regularity in repeated
reasoning.**

Attend to precision.

A door cannot function without a frame. The frame is the support system that holds the door in place. The two SMP that serve as the frame of the door are the following:

1. Make sense of problems and persevere in solving them.
5. Use appropriate tools strategically.

The threshold is another integral part of a door. The function of the threshold is to provide a transition between the inside and the outside or between rooms. SMP #6, "**Attend to precision**," serves as the threshold for the SMP doorway to the CCSSM. It is through precise and effective communication that students are able to gain insights about how they think about mathematics. As NCTM states in *PSSM*, "It is important to give students experiences that help them appreciate the power and precision of mathematical language" (2005, p. 63).

If a door is locked, keys are required to gain entry. Being the guardian of the keys was historically a very high honor and came with great responsibility. The key to unlocking the door of the SMP is being deliberate and intentional in their implementation. It is one thing to say the SMPs are embedded in daily instruction. It is another to actually seamlessly interweave the mathematical practices with content instruction. The following strategies will aid in unlocking, opening, and successfully going through the doorway of the Standards for Mathematical Practice to implement the CCSSM effectively.

Strategies Matrix

	Strategies	SMP #1 Make sense of problems and persevere in solving them.	SMP #2 Reason abstractly and quantitatively.	SMP #3 Construct viable arguments and critique the reasoning of others.	SMP #4 Model with mathematics.	SMP #5 Use appropriate tools strategically.	SMP #6 Attend to precision.	SMP #7 Look for and make use of structure.	SMP #8 Look for and express regularity in repeated reasoning.
Framing Strategies	Problem-Solving Process	✓	✓	✓	✓	✓	✓	✓	✓
Framing Strategies	Visual Vocabulary	✓	✓	✓	✓	✓	✓	✓	✓
Framing Strategies	Puzzling Problems	✓	✓	✓	✓	✓	✓	✓	✓
Strategies	ABC Sum Race	✓		✓		✓	✓		
Strategies	Grid Games	✓	✓	✓	✓	✓	✓		
Strategies	Matching Mania	✓	✓	✓	✓	✓	✓	✓	✓
Strategies	Walk This Way	✓	✓	✓		✓	✓	✓	✓
Strategies	What's My Move?	✓	✓	✓	✓	✓	✓	✓	✓

SECTION 2

---◼---

Framing Strategies for Implementing SMPs #1, #5, and #6

The following three Standards for Mathematical Practice, SMP #1, SMP #5, and SMP #6, serve as the frame for the door. Students who venture through this door are on a journey that promotes processes, proficiencies, and practices in the Common Core mathematics classroom. These three practices are pivotal because they not only develop conceptual understanding of the content, but also because they play an integral role in the implementation of the other five practices. These practices should permeate the mathematics classroom environment and become part of the daily fabric of both mathematics instruction and the students' mathematics experience.

1. Make sense of problems and persevere in solving them.

Mathematically proficient students start by explaining to themselves the meaning of a problem and looking for entry points to its solution. They analyze givens, constraints, relationships, and goals. They make conjectures about the form and meaning of the solution and plan a solution pathway rather than simply jumping into a solution attempt. They consider analogous problems, and try special cases and simpler forms of the original problem in order to gain insight into its solution. They monitor and evaluate their progress and change course if necessary. Older students might, depending on the context of the problem, transform algebraic expressions or change the viewing window on their graphing calculator to get the information they need. Mathematically proficient students can explain correspondences between equations, verbal descriptions, tables, and graphs or draw diagrams of important features and relationships, graph data, and search for regularity or trends. Younger students might rely on using concrete objects or pictures to help conceptualize and solve a problem. Mathematically proficient students check their answers to problems using a different method, and they continually ask themselves, "Does this make sense?" They can understand the approaches of others to solving complex problems and identify correspondences between different approaches. (Common Core State Standards Initiative, 2012b)

As students move into middle grades, they begin to work with problems and tasks that require data to be collected and analyzed, an unknown quantity to be found, or a prediction to be made that connects to other disciplines. These tasks continue to support and extend the students' mathematical disposition and problem-solving skills. Tasks need to be carefully chosen to give students at all levels a point of entry and yet be both cognitively demanding and interesting enough to motivate the student to keep at it until a reasonable solution is obtained. Talking, writing, and reflecting about mathematics are just as important for middle-school students as they were for primary and elementary students. Sometimes mathematical discourse is more of a challenge at this level due to the many procedural concepts that are being introduced. Teachers must monitor this carefully.

5. Use appropriate tools strategically.

Mathematically proficient students consider the available tools when solving a mathematical problem. These tools might include pencil and paper, concrete models, a ruler, a protractor, a calculator, a spreadsheet, a computer algebra system, a statistical package, or dynamic geometry software. Proficient students are sufficiently familiar with tools appropriate for their grade or course to make sound decisions about when each of these tools might be helpful, recognizing both the insight to be gained and their limitations. For example, mathematically proficient high school students analyze graphs of functions and solutions generated using a graphing calculator. They detect possible errors by strategically using estimation and other mathematical knowledge. When making mathematical models, they know that technology can enable them to visualize the results of varying assumptions, explore consequences, and compare predictions with data. Mathematically proficient students at various grade levels are able to identify relevant external mathematical resources, such as digital content located on a website, and use them to pose or solve problems. They are able to use technological tools to explore and deepen their understanding of concepts. (Common Core State Standards Initiative, 2012b)

A tool is some type of device that allows a person to carry out a particular function. There are many tools that can be used in a middle-school mathematics classroom. Everything from paper and pencil to manipulatives to various forms of technology, including calculators and dynamic computer software, can be thought of as a tool. These become tools of investigation for students as they are doing mathematics. Students need to experience mathematics, and the use of tools of investigation allows them that experience. Middle-school students continue to add appropriate tools to their elementary toolbox, which contained the various tools that were available to them in K–5. The use of fraction tiles and Cuisenaire® rods in elementary grades is now extended to a more strategic use of algebra tiles or algebra blocks in modeling and working with expressions and equations. Students understand how to use these new tools effectively and know when and why it is more efficient and strategic to use each tool. Students need to know and understand the benefits as well as the limitations of various tools. They need to recognize that tools are a way to explore and deepen their understanding of various concepts. Students also need to be able to use estimation to check the reasonableness of an answer.

6. Attend to precision.
Mathematically proficient students try to communicate precisely to others. They try to use clear definitions in discussion with others and in their own reasoning. They state the meaning of the symbols they choose, including using the equal sign consistently and appropriately. They are careful about specifying units of measure, and labeling axes to clarify the correspondence with quantities in a problem. They calculate accurately and efficiently, express numerical answers with a degree of precision appropriate for the problem context. In the elementary grades, students give carefully formulated explanations to each other. By the time they reach high school they have learned to examine claims and make explicit use of definitions. (Common Core State Standards Initiative, 2012b)

NCTM considers communication

a way of sharing ideas and clarifying understanding. Through communication, ideas become objects of reflection, refinement, discussion, and amendment. The communication process also helps build meaning and permanence for ideas and makes them public. When students are challenged to think and reason about mathematics and to communicate the results of their thinking to others orally or in writing, they learn to be clear and convincing. (NCTM, 2005, p. 60)

Communication can be oral or written: it can employ a visual model or graphic. Students should not memorize a definition just to spit it out again. The purpose of learning vocabulary is to use it later to facilitate building the structures of mathematics. Vocabulary in any discipline usually has connotations specific for that discipline. That is one of the challenges in a technical subject such as mathematics. However, the teacher is the person responsible for monitoring students' precise use of vocabulary, units of measure, symbols, and other mathematical language.

Students who are mathematically proficient and use clear and concise vocabulary, symbol notation, and units are the students who gain deeper insights into the mathematics they are studying. Middle-school students may still need to discuss and communicate with drawings and concrete models before moving to symbolic or abstract representations. They need to be encouraged to continue to write about mathematics. Oral discussions, concrete models, and drawings need to build naturally to writing about their investigations and reasoning. As students practice and continue on their journey through mathematics, they will develop better communication skills and more formal approaches to their writing and justifications, if guided. Students will begin to use more mathematically precise language as they critique their peers' work and engage in discussions. The simple familiar language used in early grades begins to give way to the more formal language of mathematics in the middle-school grades.

The Strategies

The following three strategies illustrate how these three practices permeate the other five.

- **Problem-Solving Process** offers a graphic organizer and an approach for solving problems that can make contextual problem solving accessible to diverse students.
- **Visual Vocabulary** offers strategies for students to go beyond rote memorization of words to developing true understanding of mathematical terms, symbols, and notations. It employs forming concepts, comparing and contrasting concepts, and using a graphic organizer.
- **Puzzling Problems** offers a nonthreatening environment in which students can approach and engage in contextual problem solving while working cooperatively or independently.

Problem-Solving Process

———■———

Overview

"Problem solving means engaging in a task for which the solution method is not known in advance" (NCTM, 2005, p. 52).

The first Standard for Mathematical Practice is "Make sense of problems and persevere in solving them" (Common Core State Standards Initiative, 2012b). Problem solving has traditionally been a challenge for many students, whether in the primary grades or in high school. Knowing "how to teach" problem solving can be an equal challenge for the teacher. One of the difficulties when facilitating problem solving lies in the variety of problems that students encounter as well as the multiple strategies that can be applied to solving them. Another obstacle facing teachers and students is the reading that is required for "making sense of problems." For some students, this is the first roadblock in finding that "entry point" to engage in the problem.

In *Principles and Standards for School Mathematics*, NCTM goes on to state that students should be able to do the following:

♦ build new mathematical knowledge through problem solving
♦ solve problems that arise in mathematics and in other contexts
♦ apply and adapt a variety of appropriate strategies to solve problems
♦ monitor and reflect on the process of mathematical problem solving (NCTM, 2005, p. 116)

Probably the most universally recognized "problem-solving process" can be attributed to George Pôlya, the Hungarian mathematician who came to America in 1940 and published *How to Solve It* in 1943. *How to Solve It* is a small book in which Pôlya describes several methods for solving problems, not just problems in mathematics. Pôlya suggests the following "four-step" plan:

♦ understand the problem
♦ devise a plan

♦ carry out the plan
♦ review or extend the work

These four steps are fluid, as illustrated by the graphical adaptation of Pôlya's plan.

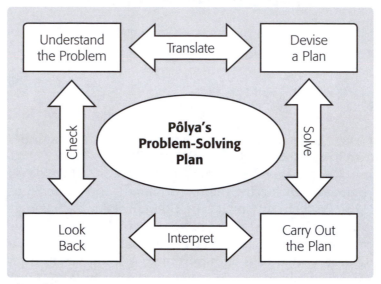

Adapted by Tammy L. Jones
TLJ Consulting Group

If you cannot devise an effective plan, back up and check for understanding of the problem. Once you have reached a solution, look back and reflect to check for the reasonableness of the answer. These four steps have been adapted as illustrated and defined below in a five-step process.

Directions

The following is a problem-solving process that can be used to assist students in making sense of problems **(Practice #1)** as well as decontextualizing and contextualizing word problems **(Practice #2)**. The process also requires students to construct viable arguments **(Practice #3)** as they formulate their own ideas about the meaning of the problem and make predictions about the outcome. Once they obtain a solution, students compare it to the prediction to determine the reasonableness of the solution. By following explicit steps to unpack the problem, students are able to begin the process with minimal to no teacher guidance and complete the initial steps. This eliminates the blank piece of paper or the famous "I don't know" answer. Using a consistent process over time will assist students in becoming better problem solvers. While this process may not always fit every problem, it does help students develop a systematic approach to finding the entry point into various tasks.

Five-Step Problem-Solving Process

A reproducible version of this tool is available in Appendix A (pp. 93–94).

1. **Answer Statement**
   a. The question usually appears as the last sentence of the problem. Students can cover the other information and focus on the last line to determine what the problem is asking. (If the question is not here, students can check each preceding line until it is found.)
   b. Students write the question as an answer statement and leave a blank for the solution.
2. **Given Information**
   a. Students use the same process of viewing each sentence separately, covering everything else.
   b. Students determine and record relevant information from the problem.
3. **Strategy/Plan**
   a. Students use this space to state additional ideas they have about the problem, such as other information they know about the problem, possible strategies for getting started, estimations for the solution, constraints, or predictions.
   b. This is the section that allows students to formulate their own ideas about the problem and provides a place for them to create their own meaning about what is being asked.
4. **Solve**
   a. Students select a strategy (translate verbal statements into mathematical statements, draw a picture, make a table, etc.) and solve.
   b. Students can compare their solution to the estimation to determine the reasonableness of their answer.

5. **Check**
   a. Students check their answers by substitution or by using another method to justify.
   b. Once the answer has been checked, students write the answer in the blank from step #1.

———◼———

Common Core State Standards for Mathematics Addressed

Solve real-world and mathematical problems involving area, surface area, and volume.

CCSS.Math.Content.6.G.A.2 Find the volume of a right rectangular prism with fractional edge lengths by packing it with unit cubes of the appropriate unit fraction edge lengths, and show that the volume is the same as would be found by multiplying the edge lengths of the prism. Apply the formulas $V = lwh$ and $V = bh$ to find volumes of right rectangular prisms with fractional edge lengths in the context of solving real-world and mathematical problems.

Solve real-life and mathematical problems involving angle measure, area, surface area, and volume.

CCSS.Math.Content.7.G.B.4 Know the formulas for the area and circumference of a circle and use them to solve problems; give an informal derivation of the relationship between the circumference and area of a circle.

CCSS.Math.Content.7.G.B.6 Solve real-world and mathematical problems involving area, volume, and surface area of two- and three-dimensional objects composed of triangles, quadrilaterals, polygons, cubes, and right prisms.

Solve real-world and mathematical problems involving volume of cylinders, cones, and spheres.

CCSS.Math.Content.8.G.C.9 Know the formulas for the volumes of cones, cylinders, and spheres and use them to solve real-world and mathematical problems.

(Common Core State Standards Initiative, 2012a)

———◼———

Problem-Solving Process Example

In middle school, students build on their prior experiences with measurement and geometric figures from the elementary grades. They continue to touch, see, measure, model, and manipulate figures as they investigate properties of both two- and three-dimensional shapes. The study of geometry provides a rich environment in which middle-school students can further develop mathematical reasoning, both inductively and deductively. Students conjecture about circles and polygons, nets composed of those shapes that can be used to build solids, and surface areas and volumes of those solids. The real world provides many contexts for investigations.

Problem Statement

Mrs. Jones gave each of her students a standard piece of cardstock. She told them to use it to model a cylinder. Patrick and Jamal each rolled up his piece of cardstock to form a cylinder. The two cylinders that Patrick and Jamal made were different. Mrs. Jones asked the two students to hypothesize whose cylinder would have the greatest volume. Jamal thought his cylinder had a greater volume than Patrick's. Mrs. Jones then asked the students to determine the volume of their cylinders. Sketch a picture of the two cylinders Jamal and Patrick could have made. What information about their cylinders do Patrick and Jamal need in order to determine their volumes? Label that information on your sketch. If Jamal was NOT correct in his hypothesis, which cylinder could have been his? Justify your answer.

Guided Facilitation

NOTE: This is a good example to discuss different types of questions that can be asked in a problem and what is required to arrive at a solution. And this is a multistep problem.

1. **Answer Statement**
    Have the students look for the question marks to find the questions. Discuss the questions so they understand how to rephrase them as statements such as "The information needed to determine the volume of the cylinder is _____ " and "The cylinder that was Jamal's is _____ because _____ ."

2. **Given Information**
    Guide students to model what Patrick and Jamal did by rolling up a piece of paper. Check their ability to draw cylinders that model the two possibilities. It would be interesting to have students choose at this point which cylinder they think would be Jamal's before moving on.

    Check for appropriate labeling of units and their drawing to get an idea of their spatial sense development. Having some students measure in inches and some in centimeters or even millimeters can easily differentiate this activity as well as allow students to experience measurements in different systems as well as different forms of rational numbers.

3. **Strategy/Plan**

   For this piece of the problem, students should be able to state how to find the volume of a right rectangular solid. Using the basic volume formula $V = Bh$, where B represents the area of the base of the solid, allows students to connect to prior learning on the area of different figures and to extend the formula to solids with circular bases. This is also a good place to check students' understanding of what is "needed" information for this piece of the problem versus what is not needed. (Note: "b" is used to identify the length base of a polygonal shape where "B" is used to identify the area of the base of the solid.)

4. **Solve**

   Here is an example of a problem that does not have "a solution" as such. The students must determine the volume for each of the cylinders, make a comparison, and then justify their decision. Students can find the "exact" volumes by leaving π as part of the answer, or they can find an approximation for the volumes by using the traditional approximations for π, $^{22}/_7$, or 3.14.

5. **Check**

   This is a very important step in the problem-solving process. Checking for the reasonableness of the answer is a skill that can be developed only through repeated practice. Let students compare their answers in English standard measurements as well as in metric measurements. Ask students if their guess as to which cylinder was Jamal's was correct or not. As an extension, you could ask students to conjecture about the possibility that Jamal's and Patrick's cylinders could have exactly the same volume.

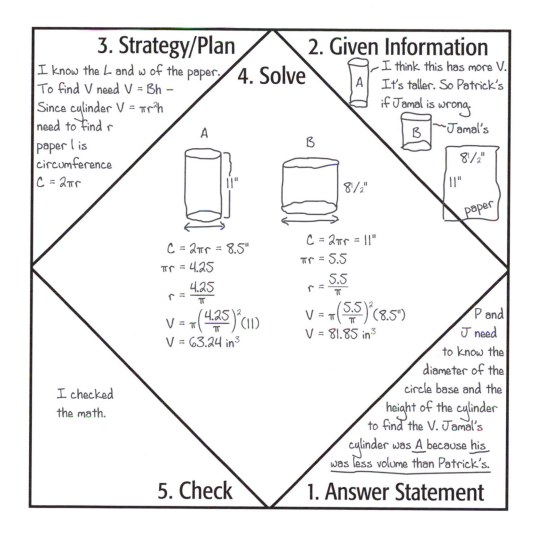

3. Strategy/Plan

I know the L and w of the paper. To find V need V = Bh – Since cylinder V = πr²h need to find r paper l is circumference C = 2πr

4. Solve

2. Given Information

I think this has more V. It's taller. So Patrick's if Jamal is wrong.

A

~Jamal's

B

8½"

11"

paper

A

11"

$C = 2\pi r = 8.5"$
$\pi r = 4.25$
$r = \dfrac{4.25}{\pi}$
$V = \pi\left(\dfrac{4.25}{\pi}\right)^2(11)$
$V = 63.24 \text{ in}^3$

B

8½"

$C = 2\pi r = 11"$
$\pi r = 5.5$
$r = \dfrac{5.5}{\pi}$
$V = \pi\left(\dfrac{5.5}{\pi}\right)^2(8.5")$
$V = 81.85 \text{ in}^3$

P and J need to know the diameter of the circle base and the height of the cylinder to find the V. Jamal's cylinder was A because his was less volume than Patrick's.

I checked the math.

5. Check

1. Answer Statement

Alternate Problem

Mrs. Jones gave each of her students a standard piece of cardstock. She told them they were going to make a rectangular solid—without a top. Each group was to cut out a square with the side length given in the table below from each of the four corners of the cardstock. They then were to make a box by turning up the four flaps and taping them in the four corners.

Group	Side of the square cut out from each corner	Group	Side of the square cut out from each corner
A	½ inch	E	3 inches
B	1 inch	F	2 cm
C	1½ inches	G	5 cm
D	2 inches	H	8 cm

Once each group had made its box, Mrs. Jones asked the students to hypothesize whose box would have the greatest volume. Group D thinks its box has the greatest volume. Mrs. Jones then asked the students to determine the volume of their boxes. Sketch a picture of the boxes that would have been made. What information do the groups need about their boxes in order to determine their volumes? Label that information on your sketch. If Group D was NOT correct in its hypothesis, which group's box could have the greatest volume? Justify your answer.

Extension

Once students have collected the data and determined the volume of the boxes, they can graph the length of the side of the square cut out and the volume of the box. Making connections between the graph and the information the students collected can lead to rich discussions about nonlinear graphs. Students are usually amazed that the metric and English standard measures fit together so well on the graphs. Again, this can lead to rich discussions about conversions between systems and conversion factors.

Ideas for Implementing the Five-Step Process Template

♦ Individual: Each student is assigned a problem and completes the chart individually as classwork or homework.

♦ Individual/Pairs: Students are given a completed chart and must create the problem scenario.

♦ Individual/Pairs: Work three or four problems using the five-step process. Cut the steps of each problem into individual strips and place in an envelope. Give students the envelope and ask them to reassemble the strips to form the problems and solution pathways.

♦ Individual/Pairs: Give students a completed chart that contains errors and have them identify the errors and make corrections.

♦ Partner Pairs: Think-Pair-Share. Allow an initial period of time for each student to read and understand the problem. Then allow partners to discuss and solve the problem together. Students should be prepared to explain their solution to the class.

♦ Partner Pairs: Same as above, except that students must solve the problem from two solution pathways.

♦ Partner Pairs: Each partner completes steps 1-4 of their individually assigned problem. Partners will then exchange papers and complete step 5 by checking the answer.

♦ Small Group: Each student begins with a problem and does step 1. Upon completion of that step, students hand their paper to the next person in a clockwise (or counterclockwise) rotation. Each student then completes the next step in the problem. The process continues for three more steps until all of the steps of the process have been completed.

Visual Vocabulary

Overview

Building mathematical vocabulary is essential, not just for English Language Learners but for all students. Vocabulary is the foundation upon which mathematical understandings develop. Precise use of mathematical vocabulary, symbols, and notations is foundational to successfully implementing all of the Standards for Mathematical Practice. This strategy involves students representing their understanding of vocabulary words, phrases, and symbols. The idea was adapted from a lesson shared by Julia Hayes, Newport News, Virginia.

Directions

- Teams will be given a card identifying a math-related word or phrase. If the classroom has a topical word wall, these words or phrases will come from there.
- Teams will illustrate the concept or meaning of the word or phrase without using numbers, variables, or other words. This is *not* Pictionary®: the illustrations should convey meaning, not clues for "guessing the word."
- A gallery walk will be conducted to identify the words. The drawings can be numbered and the students can record the number and the word or phrase they believe is being represented.
- Drawings will be posted. Placing these with the words from the word wall will allow students to continue working with these throughout the next unit as well. Students could also replicate these in their student mathematics glossary they are developing.

Common Core State Standards for Mathematics Addressed

Solve real-world and mathematical problems involving area, surface area, and volume.

CCSS.Math.Content.6.G.A.2 Find the volume of a right rectangular prism with fractional edge lengths by packing it with unit cubes of the appropriate unit fraction edge lengths, and show that the volume is the same as would be found by multiplying the edge lengths of the prism. Apply the formulas $V = lwh$ and $V = bh$ to find volumes of right rectangular prisms with fractional edge lengths in the context of solving real-world and mathematical problems.

Understand ratio concepts and use ratio reasoning to solve problems.

CCSS.Math.Content.6.RP.A.1 Understand the concept of a ratio and use ratio language to describe a ratio relationship between two quantities. *For example, "The ratio of wings to beaks in the bird house at the zoo was 2:1, because for every 2 wings there was 1 beak." "For every vote candidate A received, candidate C received nearly three votes."*

CCSS.Math.Content.6.RP.A.2 Understand the concept of a unit rate a/b associated with a ratio a:b with b ≠ 0, and use rate language in the context of a ratio relationship. *For example, "This recipe has a ratio of 3 cups of flour to 4 cups of sugar, so there is ¾ cup of flour for each cup of sugar." "We paid $75 for 15 hamburgers, which is a rate of $5 per hamburger."*[1]

Solve real-life and mathematical problems involving angle measure, area, surface area, and volume.

CCSS.Math.Content.7.G.B.4 Know the formulas for the area and circumference of a circle and use them to solve problems; give an informal derivation of the relationship between the circumference and area of a circle.

CCSS.Math.Content.7.G.B.6 Solve real-world and mathematical problems involving area, volume and surface area of two- and three-dimensional objects composed of triangles, quadrilaterals, polygons, cubes, and right prisms.

Analyze proportional relationships and use them to solve real-world and mathematical problems.
CCSS.Math.Content.7.RP.A.2 Recognize and represent proportional relationships between quantities.

Solve real-world and mathematical problems involving volume of cylinders, cones, and spheres.
CCSS.Math.Content.8.G.C.9 Know the formulas for the volumes of cones, cylinders, and spheres and use them to solve real-world and mathematical problems.

(Common Core State Standards Initiative, 2012a)

Examples

The examples below illustrate two different math words or phrases.

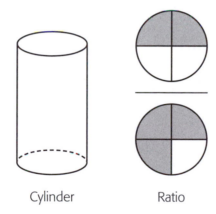

Cylinder   Ratio

Guided Facilitation

Assessment Activity
1. Upon completing the vocabulary illustration activity, create a set of cards displaying the vocabulary word or phrase, a visual representation of the word or phrase, and its definition.
2. Give each student (or group of students) a set of cards.
3. Students must match their cards appropriately.

Vocabulary Word or Phrase	Visual Representation	Definition

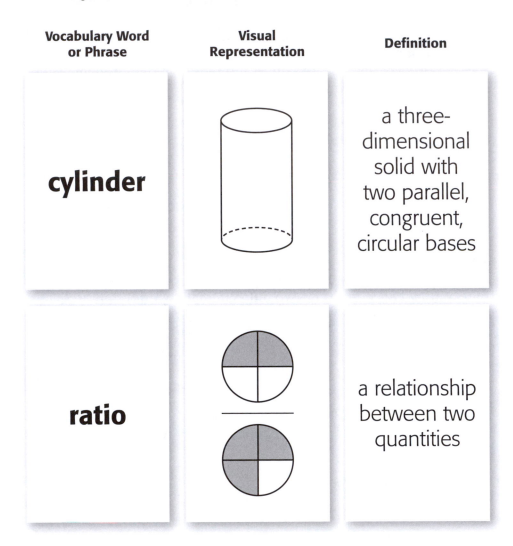

Extension Activity

1. Once the students have matched their cards correctly, they will record the vocabulary word or phrase, the visual representation of the word or phrase, and its definition using a vocabulary concept map, such as a Frayer model.

2. Students will then define characteristics of the word or phrase and create a visual counterexample. (At this point, students are allowed to use numerical, algebraic, or symbolic representations.)

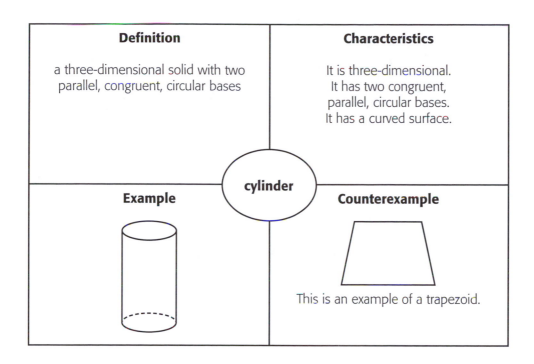

Definition	Characteristics
a three-dimensional solid with two parallel, congruent, circular bases	It is three-dimensional. It has two congruent, parallel, circular bases. It has a curved surface.

cylinder

Example	Counterexample
	This is an example of a trapezoid.

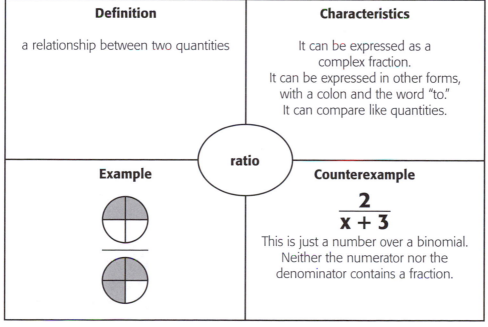

Definition	Characteristics
a relationship between two quantities	It can be expressed as a complex fraction. It can be expressed in other forms, with a colon and the word "to." It can compare like quantities.

ratio

Example	Counterexample
	$$\frac{2}{x+3}$$ This is just a number over a binomial. Neither the numerator nor the denominator contains a fraction.

A blank reproducible version of this tool is available in Appendix A (p. 95).

Puzzling Problems

Overview

Puzzling Problems involves students in cooperative groups working on basic problem solving or a rich task that involves multiple components. The sample tasks that have been developed illustrate the latter. The problems are scaffolded so each subsequent question in some part depends upon the students completing the prior piece. These problems were developed to model what a performance-based assessment at a higher cognitive level might look like. Writing is a key component in each of these problems. This is a perfect opportunity for students to employ math journaling or a Mathematician's Notebook to individually record their observations, reasoning, and thoughts as they work through each component of the problems. It also gives them a reference for the next component of the task. Teachers need to remember that just because students can discuss something verbally does not necessarily mean they can capture those thoughts in written words. Writing in mathematics needs to be a natural, daily part of a student's experiences.

This strategy provides students the opportunity to work through mathematical problems collaboratively. The idea was adapted from a lesson shared by Bob Trammel, a math consultant in Indiana.

Directions

1. Enlarge a word problem or task to fit on one sheet of cardstock. Cut the problem into puzzle pieces. The number of pieces can correspond to the number of students per group, or you can give each student multiple pieces of the same puzzle.
2. Give each student a puzzle piece or pieces.
3. Students must match their puzzle pieces to form a problem to solve.
4. As a learning group, students select a strategy to solve the problem.
5. Students solve the problem as a team and submit a solution. The team must be able to construct a viable argument for their solution and document it individually as a journal activity.

If you would like to have the teams solve more than one problem, place additional puzzles around the room and have teams rotate until they have solved the number of problems you determine. Rich tasks can also be broken down so the first problem is the beginning of the task and subsequent problems are the rest of the task.

Common Core State Standards for Mathematics Addressed

Develop understanding of statistical variability.

CCSS.Math.Content.6.SP.A.2 Understand that a set of data collected to answer a statistical question has a distribution, which can be described by its center, spread, and overall shape.

CCSS.Math.Content.6.SP.A.3 Recognize that a measure of center for a numerical data set summarizes all of its values with a single number, while a measure of variation describes how its values vary with a single number.

Summarize and describe distributions.

CCSS.Math.Content.6.SP.B.5 Summarize numerical data sets in relation to their context, such as by:

CCSS.Math.Content.6.SP.B.5c Giving quantitative measures of center (median and/or mean) and variability (interquartile range and/or mean absolute deviation), as well as describing any overall pattern and any striking deviations from the overall pattern with reference to the context in which the data were gathered.

CCSS.Math.Content.6.SP.B.5d Relating the choice of measures of center and variability to the shape of the data distribution and the context in which the data were gathered.

Investigate chance processes and develop, use, and evaluate probability models.

CCSS.Math.Content.7.SP.C.5 Understand that the probability of a chance event is a number between 0 and 1 that expresses the likelihood of the event occurring. Larger numbers indicate greater likelihood. A probability near 0 indicates an unlikely event, a probability around ½ indicates an event that is neither unlikely nor likely, and a probability near 1 indicates a likely event.

CCSS.Math.Content.7.SP.C.6 Approximate the probability of a chance event by collecting data on the chance process that produces it and observing its long-run relative frequency, and predict the approximate relative frequency given the probability. *For example, when rolling a number cube 600 times, predict that a 3 or 6 would be rolled roughly 200 times, but probably not exactly 200 times.*

Solve real-life and mathematical problems involving angle measure, area, surface area, and volume.

CCSS.Math.Content.7.G.B.4 Know the formulas for the area and circumference of a circle and use them to solve problems; give an informal derivation of the relationship between the circumference and area of a circle.

Investigate patterns of association in bivariate data.

CCSS.Math.Content.8.SP.A.1 Construct and interpret scatter plots for bivariate measurement data to investigate patterns of association between two quantities. Describe patterns such as clustering, outliers, positive or negative association, linear association, and nonlinear association.

CCSS.Math.Content.8.SP.A.2 Know that straight lines are widely used to model relationships between two quantitative variables. For scatter plots that suggest a linear association, informally fit a straight line, and informally assess the model fit by judging the closeness of the data points to the line.

CCSS.Math.Content.8.SP.A.3 Use the equation of a linear model to solve problems in the context of bivariate measurement data, interpreting the slope and intercept. *For example, in a linear model for a biology experiment, interpret a slope of 1.5 cm/hr as meaning that an additional hour of sunlight each day is associated with an additional 1.5 cm in mature plant height.*

(Common Core State Standards Initiative, 2012a)

Grade 6 Example

Dave was shown the following data set:

$$92, 73, 86, 99, 85, 75$$

Determine the three measures of central tendency for this data set and explain their meaning with reference to the data set.

Looking at Dave's data set, list at least two real-life contexts in which these numbers could exist. Explain each of the measures of central tendency in context.

What would happen to each measure of central tendency if another number, 60, were added to the set? Explain your reasoning.

Thinking about what each of the measures of central tendency describes, list three numbers that could be added to the data set so:

a.   the median does not change
b.   the mean does not change
c.   the mode does not change

Explain fully why there is no change in each of the three measures. Describe numbers that would change the three measures and explain why.

A reproducible version of this tool is available in Appendix A (p. 96).

Grade 7 Example

Jamal used a spinner file he had on his handheld. The spinner is shown below.

Trials: 0

What is the probability of the spinner landing on each of the colored sections? Explain your thinking. Are there any values that could not be used to represent the probabilities? Why or why not?

Draw a circle graph showing what you predict the outcome would be for 10 spins.

Jamal set the program to spin the spinner 10 times. His results are shown in the picture on the right.

Trials: 10

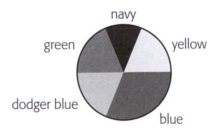

Results

How do these results compare to yours? Write a couple of statements about the differences and the reasons for these differences. Why were not all 8 colors shown?

Write a statement about what you think the results would look like for 100 spins, and explain your reasoning.

Jamal did set the program to spin 100 times.

Trials: 100   **Results**

How do these results compare to yours? Write a couple of statements about the differences and the reasons for these differences. If you ran the simulation, how do you think your results would compare with Jamal's? Why?

Write a statement about what you think the results would look like for 1,000 spins, and explain your reasoning.

Is there a number of trials you could set the simulation for so the results would always be the same? Why or why not?

A reproducible version of this tool is available in Appendix A (pp. 97–98).

Grade 8 Example

Students in a middle-school class measured 10 circular objects and recorded their measurements below.

Object #	Circumference	Diameter
1	25 inches	$7\frac{1}{2}$ inches
2	8 inches	$2\frac{1}{2}$ inches
3	$4\frac{1}{2}$ inches	$1\frac{1}{2}$ inches
4	13 inches	4 inches
5	22 inches	$6\frac{1}{2}$ inches
6	68 inches	22 inches
7	14 inches	$4\frac{1}{2}$ inches
8	11 inches	$3\frac{1}{2}$ inches
9	$28\frac{1}{2}$ inches	9 inches
10	47 inches	15 inches

Create a scatter plot of the data. Discuss your observations about the scatter plot. Be specific.

Using the scatterplot created in part 1, fit a line to the scatterplot and assess the fit. Justify your reasoning. Identify the key features of the line used in your model. Discuss the relationship between the key features in the model and how those features relate to the context of the data.

What key feature of the model relates the circumference of a circle to its diameter?

How close was the students' collected data to the actual accepted model for the circumference of a circle?

Why do you think there was a difference?

Would it have mattered if the measurements had been in metric units?

What is the relationship between the area of a circle and the circle's diameter?

A reproducible version of this tool is available in Appendix A (p. 99).

Guided Facilitation

Multiple Representations
1. For each unit of study, create a set of puzzles. Each puzzle will contain multiple pieces with each piece displaying a different representation of the same problem.
2. Place students in groups of two or three. Each group will receive a set of puzzle pieces.
3. Students must match their pieces appropriately to solve the set of puzzles.

Puzzle Piece Sort (Classification)
1. For each unit of study, create a set of puzzles pieces. Each puzzle piece will display a different mathematical example.
2. Place students in groups of two or three. Each group will receive a set of puzzle pieces.
3. Students must sort and classify all their puzzle pieces.

Equivalency Match
1. For each unit of study, create a set of puzzles. Each puzzle will comprise two pieces.
2. Each piece of the puzzle will display a different representation of an equivalent quantity.
3. Each pair of students will receive a set of puzzles.
4. Students complete all the puzzles appropriately to show matching equivalencies.

Process Statements
1. Choose several problems organized around one common concept. Work through each problem.
2. Create a puzzle for each problem. Each piece of the puzzle will display a different step in solving the problem from problem statement to solution.
3. Place students in groups of two or three. Each group will receive a set of puzzles.
4. Students complete all the puzzles appropriately to display the problem, process statements, and solution.

---◆---

Strategies for Implementing Combinations of SMPs

The following five Standards for Mathematical Practice, SMP #2, SMP #3, SMP #4, SMP #7, and SMP #8, serve as the door. Your students' mathematics journey continues as they apply these practices, which continue to promote processes, proficiencies, and conceptual understanding in the Common Core mathematics classroom. The implementation of these five practices often occurs in tandem as they are integrated into daily content explorations.

2. Reason abstractly and quantitatively.
Mathematically proficient students make sense of quantities and their relationships in problem situations. They bring two complementary abilities to bear on problems involving quantitative relationships: the ability to *decontextualize*—to abstract a given situation and represent it symbolically and manipulate the representing symbols as if they have a life of their own, without necessarily attending to their referents—and the ability to *contextualize*, to pause as needed during the manipulation process in order to probe into the referents for the symbols involved. Quantitative reasoning entails habits of creating a coherent representation of the problem at hand; considering the units involved; attending to the meaning of quantities, not just how to compute them; and knowing and flexibly using different properties of operations and objects. (Common Core State Standards Initiative, 2012b)

By middle school, students should be using mathematics to solve problems in other contexts regularly. It is important that they have built measurement landmarks during their elementary years and solid basic problem-solving skills. Students should be able to estimate a reasonable answer, know what operations and properties would be efficient in reaching a solution, and understand that the operations they choose represent their strategy for reaching a solution. Students need to be able to move seamlessly between the context and the quantities given in the problem and understand the mathematical symbols involved.

3. Construct viable arguments and critique the reasoning of others.
Mathematically proficient students understand and use stated assumptions, definitions, and previously established results in constructing arguments. They make conjectures and build a logical progression of statements to explore the truth of their conjectures. They are able to analyze situations by breaking them into cases, and can recognize and use counterexamples. They justify their conclusions, communicate them to others, and respond to the arguments of others. They reason inductively about data, making plausible arguments that take into account the context from which the data arose. Mathematically proficient students are also able to compare

the effectiveness of two plausible arguments, distinguish correct logic or reasoning from that which is flawed, and—if there is a flaw in an argument—explain what it is. Elementary students can construct arguments using concrete referents such as objects, drawings, diagrams, and actions. Such arguments can make sense and be correct, even though they are not generalized or made formal until later grades. Later, students learn to determine domains to which an argument applies. Students at all grades can listen or read the arguments of others, decide whether they make sense, and ask useful questions to clarify or improve the arguments. (Common Core State Standards Initiative, 2012b)

Mathematical discourse in middle school should be more complex than it was in the previous years. It should also be more abstract as students have developed deeper understanding of basic mathematical concepts as well as matured in their reasoning abilities. Middle-school students should be able to defend their work and give valid arguments to support what they did. They should also be able to evaluate their peers' work. This work needs to take place within a community of learning in which all students have the right and the responsibility to share their ideas and thoughts. Writing still plays an important role in middle school. Students should be able to write more formal explanations and supports for the strategies they have used in their investigations. Students should also be able to ask more probing questions as they engage in mathematical discourse. Teachers need to make both oral and written communication a priority and monitor it carefully.

4. Model with mathematics.
Mathematically proficient students can apply the mathematics they know to solve problems arising in everyday life, society, and the workplace. In early grades, this might be as simple as writing an addition equation to describe a situation. In middle grades, a student might apply proportional reasoning to plan a school event or analyze a problem in the community. By high school, a student might use geometry to solve a design problem or use a function to describe how one quantity of interest depends on another. Mathematically proficient students who can apply what they know are comfortable making assumptions and approximations to simplify a complicated situation, realizing that these may need revision later. They are able to identify important quantities in a practical situation and map their relationships using such tools as diagrams, two-way tables, graphs, flowcharts and formulas. They can analyze those relationships mathematically to draw conclusions. They routinely interpret their mathematical results in the context of the situation and reflect on whether the results make sense, possibly

improving the model if it has not served its purpose. (Common Core State Standards Initiative, 2012b)

As with SMP #2, students in middle school should begin to see the power of mathematics in explaining the world around them. While in elementary school, students modeled contextual situations with basic mathematical models. In middle school, student models should become more sophisticated; with the study of data analysis and statistics and probability, more meaningful mathematical investigations can be utilized. Students should be able to critique their model and see if it needs to be refined. They move fluidly between different representations of mathematics and use multiple representations when presenting their findings.

7. Look for and make use of structure.
Mathematically proficient students look closely to discern a pattern or structure. Young students, for example, might notice that three and seven more is the same amount as seven and three more, or they may sort a collection of shapes according to how many sides the shapes have. Later, students will see 7×8 equals the well remembered $7 \times 5 + 7 \times 3$, in preparation for learning about the distributive property. In the expression $x^2 + 9x + 14$, older students can see the 14 as 2×7 and the 9 as $2 + 7$. They recognize the significance of an existing line in a geometric figure and can use the strategy of drawing an auxiliary line for solving problems. They also can step back for an overview and shift perspective. They can see complicated things, such as some algebraic expressions, as single objects or as being composed of several objects. For example, they can see $5 - 3(x - y)^2$ as 5 minus a positive number times a square and use that to realize that its value cannot be more than 5 for any real numbers x and y. (Common Core State Standards Initiative, 2012b)

Mathematics is a beautiful language that contains many basic structures and patterns. In elementary school, students should have been exposed to various basic mathematical patterns and structures. By middle school, these numerical patterns can be expanded to discovering patterns and structures within algebraic expressions and the set of integers. Again, these patterns and structures help the students build the fluency they need to move on to the next level of mathematics they will encounter in high school.

8. Look for and express regularity in repeated reasoning.
Mathematically proficient students notice if calculations are repeated, and look both for general methods and for shortcuts. Upper elementary students might notice when dividing 25 by 11 that they are repeating the same calculations over and over again,

and conclude they have a repeating decimal. By paying attention to the calculation of slope as they repeatedly check whether points are on the line through (1, 2) with slope 3, middle school students might abstract the equation $(y − 2)/(x − 1) = 3$. Noticing the regularity in the way terms cancel when expanding $(x − 1)(x + 1)$, $(x − 1)(x^2 + x + 1)$, and $(x − 1)(x^3 + x2 + x + 1)$ might lead them to the general formula for the sum of a geometric series. As they work to solve a problem, mathematically proficient students maintain oversight of the process, while attending to the details. They continually evaluate the reasonableness of their intermediate results. (Common Core State Standards Initiative, 2012b)

As middle-school students explore and discover patterns in their mathematics, they should realize that these patterns represent regularities, much as they did in the study of elementary mathematics. Students can use these regularities as they reason about what strategy to employ as they are solving problems. This involves both deductive and inductive reasoning. Teachers need to provide regular experiences of both types of reasoning for their students. Mathematical discourse also needs to be a part of these experiences so students and the teacher can monitor proper use of vocabulary, symbols, operations, properties, and so on.

The Strategies

The following five strategies illustrate how these practices permeate each other.

- ◆ **Grid Games** and **Matching Mania** utilize games as a strategy for helping students gain content knowledge and understanding in a nonthreatening atmosphere. Students learn to work in cooperative group situations while practicing and strengthening their problem-solving skills.
- ◆ **The ABC Sum Race** relies on reflective discussions and journaling while students work in cooperative groups to problem-solve various tasks.
- ◆ **Walk This Way** utilizes simulations and role-playing to help students develop understanding of concepts.
- ◆ **What's My Move?** uses reflective discussions and probing questioning to develop a deeper understanding of the content being studied.

The activities in which these strategies are framed simply highlight how each strategy can be used in developing the Standards for Mathematical Practice. These strategies can be adapted to almost any content.

ABC Sum Race

Overview

This activity involves students working in groups to solve problems through a competition. The ABC Sum Race provides an opportunity for students to "construct viable arguments and critique the reasoning of others." Students work both collaboratively and individually while solving problems. Assigning students a specific letter and providing leveled problems makes the activity easily differentiable. The problems can be word problems, procedural problems, or computational problems, as desired.

The idea was adapted from a lesson shared by Susie Stark, a math teacher at Rock Island High School in Illinois.

Directions

1. Students are placed in groups of three and asked to assign each person a letter (A, B, and C) and identify a team leader.
2. The team leader comes to the front of the room and gets a task card. The task card contains three problems—problem A, B, and C.
3. Each team member solves the problem that corresponds to the letter he or she represents and records the answer on the scorecard.
4. Once all answers are recorded, the team adds the answers together to get a sum and records it on the scorecard as well. If the solutions are not able to be combined, then the Sum column is left blank.
5. The team leader brings the scorecard to the teacher to be checked. If correct, the group moves on to the next task card. If incorrect, the team must redo and resubmit.

Common Core State Standards for Mathematics Addressed

Apply and extend previous understandings of arithmetic to algebraic expressions.

CCSS.Math.Content.6.EE.A.1 Write and evaluate numerical expressions involving whole-number exponents.

CCSS.Math.Content.6.EE.A.2 Write, read, and evaluate expressions in which letters stand for numbers.

  CCSS.Math.Content.6.EE.A.2a Write expressions that record operations with numbers and with letters standing for numbers. *For example, express the calculation "Subtract y from 5" as $5 - y$.*

  CCSS.Math.Content.6.EE.A.2b Identify parts of an expression using mathematical terms (sum, term, product, factor, quotient, coefficient); view one or more parts of an expression as a single entity. *For example, describe the expression $2(8 + 7)$ as a product of two factors; view $(8 + 7)$ as both a single entity and a sum of two terms.*

  CCSS.Math.Content.6.EE.A.2c Evaluate expressions at specific values of their variables. Include expressions that arise from formulas used in real-world problems. Perform arithmetic operations, including those involving whole-number exponents, in the conventional order when there are no parentheses to specify a particular order (Order of Operations). *For example, use the formulas $V = s^3$ and $A = 6s^2$ to find the volume and surface area of a cube with sides of length $s = \frac{1}{2}$.*

Solve real-world and mathematical problems involving area, surface area, and volume.

CCSS.Math.Content.6.G.A.2 Find the volume of a right rectangular prism with fractional edge lengths by packing it with unit cubes of the appropriate unit fraction edge lengths, and show that the volume is the same as would be found by multiplying the edge lengths of the prism. Apply the formulas $V = lwh$ and $V = bh$ to find volumes of right rectangular prisms with fractional edge lengths in the context of solving real-world and mathematical problems.

CCSS.Math.Content.6.G.A.4 Represent three-dimensional figures using nets made up of rectangles and triangles, and use the nets to find the surface area of these figures. Apply these techniques in the context of solving real-world and mathematical problems.

Reason about and solve one-variable equations and inequalities.

CCSS.Math.Content.6.EE.B.5 Understand solving an equation or inequality as a process of answering a question: which values from a specified set, if any, make the equation or inequality true? Use substitution to determine whether a given number in a specified set makes an equation or inequality true.

Use properties of operations to generate equivalent expressions.

CCSS.Math.Content.7.EE.A.1 Apply properties of operations as strategies to add, subtract, factor, and expand linear expressions with rational coefficients.

Solve real-life and mathematical problems involving angle measure, area, surface area, and volume.

CCSS.Math.Content.7.G.B.6 Solve real-world and mathematical problems involving area, volume, and surface area of two- and three-dimensional objects composed of triangles, quadrilaterals, polygons, cubes, and right prisms.

Investigate chance processes and develop, use, and evaluate probability models.

CCSS.Math.Content.7.SP.C.8 Find probabilities of compound events using organized lists, tables, tree diagrams, and simulation.

CCSS.Math.Content.7.SP.C.8a Understand that, just as with simple events, the probability of a compound event is the fraction of outcomes in the sample space for which the compound event occurs.

CCSS.Math.Content.7.SP.C.8b Represent sample spaces for compound events using methods such as organized lists, tables, and tree diagrams. For an event described in everyday language (e.g., "rolling double sixes"), identify the outcomes in the sample space, which compose the event.

CCSS.Math.Content.7.SP.C.8c Design and use a simulation to generate frequencies for compound events. *For example, use random digits as a simulation tool to approximate the answer to the question: If 40% of donors have type A blood, what is the probability that it will take at least 4 donors to find one with type A blood?*

Work with radicals and integer exponents.

CCSS.Math.Content.8.EE.A.1 Know and apply the properties of integer exponents to generate equivalent numerical expressions. For example, $3^2 \times 3^{-5} = 3^{-3} = 1/3^3 = 1/27$.

Analyze and solve linear equations and pairs of simultaneous linear equations.

CCSS.Math.Content.8.EE.C.7 Solve linear equations in one variable.

CCSS.Math.Content.8.EE.C.7a Give examples of linear equations in one variable with one solution, infinitely many solutions, or no solutions. Show which of these possibilities is the case by successively transforming the given equation into simpler forms, until an equivalent equation of the form $x = a$, $a = a$, or $a = b$ results (where a and b are different numbers).

CCSS.Math.Content.8.EE.C.7b Solve linear equations with rational number coefficients, including equations whose solutions require expanding expressions using the distributive property and collecting like terms.

Understand and apply the Pythagorean Theorem.
CCSS.Math.Content.8.G.B.7 Apply the Pythagorean Theorem to determine unknown side lengths in right triangles in real-world and mathematical problems in two and three dimensions.

(Common Core State Standards Initiative, 2012a)

Examples

A. $8 + (2 \cdot 5) \times 3^4 \div 9$

B. $2^2 \cdot 20 \div 4 - 7 \cdot 3 + 55$

C. $4 - 3 [4 - 2 (6 - 3)] \div 2$

Solve for x.

A. $-2 (x - 3) - 4x = -8 + x$

B. $2x - 5 (x + 1) = 3x + 1$

C. $4x + 3 (2x - 4) = x$

Caleb has 11 red marbles, 15 green marbles, 8 yellow marbles, 5 white marbles, 9 blue marbles, and 2 black marbles in a bag. There are no other marbles in the bag.

A. What is the probability that Caleb will select at random either a red or black marble?
B. What is the probability that Caleb will select at random either a yellow or white marble?
C. What is the probability that Caleb will select at random either a green or blue marble?

Determine whether or not the triangle is a right triangle. Use the length of the hypotenuse, if it exists, as the number to create the sum. If the triangle is not a right triangle, use 0 as the number to sum.

A.   14, 48, 50

B.   12, 16, 25

C.   11, 60, 61

A.   Draw a net for a cube. How many faces does it have?

B.   A cube has a side of length 2.4 cm. Determine the surface area of the cube.

C.   A cube has a side of length 2.4 cm. Determine the volume of the cube.

A reproducible version of this tool is available in Appendix A (pp. 103–104).

ABC Sum Race Scorecard

	A	B	C	SUM
1				
2				
3				
4				
5				

A reproducible version of this tool is available in Appendix A (p. 105).

Answer Key			
A	**B**	**C**	**SUM**
1 98	54	7	159
2 $X = 2$	$X = -1$	$X = \frac{4}{3}$	$\frac{7}{3}$ or $2\frac{1}{3}$
3 $\frac{13}{15} = 0.26$ $= 26\%$	$\frac{13}{15} = 0.26$ $= 26\%$	$\frac{24}{50} = 0.48$ $= 48\%$	1 or 100%
4 Yes, 50	No, 0	Yes, 61	111
5 6	34.56 cm²	13.82 cm³	54.38

A reproducible version of this tool is available in Appendix A (p. 106).

Guided Facilitation

♦ The first time through, students must individually solve the problem that corresponds to their letter and record the answer on the answer sheet. If the group leader is sent back to the group with incorrect solutions, the entire team can work together to find the errors and resubmit.

♦ Usually, the first time the team leader submits incorrect answers, the teacher will say that the scorecard has incorrect answers, but not which parts are incorrect. The second time the scorecard is submitted with errors, the teacher will give more specific feedback, such as "Check part B."

♦ If the content is not conducive to "summing" the answers, students will leave that column on the scorecard blank or adapt it to combining like terms, etc.

♦ Color-code the task cards to keep track of which card each group is solving. If you have access to a color printer, you can color code the problem numbers on the scorecard.

♦ Set a specific length of time for students to work or call time when a group reaches the final task card. It is best to call time before the last task card is completed. This will eliminate winners and losers and ensure everyone continues to work until the end of the activity.

Grid Games

Overview

Grid Games is a strategy that creates a nonthreatening environment in which students can practice and build confidence in problem solving and procedural mathematics through a game. Playing the game itself allows students to develop their critical thinking skills while they are building strategies for capturing a cell or blocking their opponent.

Students work problems in order to cover a certain number of the cells on the grid sheet. Students can try to cover 3 in a row, 4 in a row, or even all the cells on the card to win the game as determined by the teacher.

Grid Games was developed by Melisa Rice and is being shared with permission. Additional card sets and topics can be found at www.gridgamesgalore.com.

Directions

Each activity is to be run off on cardstock. The other items necessary to play the games are counters or tiles, a number cube, and a letter cube. Use a foam cube or a cube with stick-on labels to make the letter cube. Use the letters A, B, C, D, E, and F.

1. This game is best played in pairs. Each pair of students needs the Grid Game Board for the Grid Game being played, two student recording sheets, a game sheet, a number cube and a letter cube, and counters of two different colors or double-sided counters. Spinners are also an option instead of the cubes. Provide a number spinner and a letter spinner.
2. Each player rolls the number cube. High roll is Player 1, who begins the game.
3. Player 1 rolls the two cubes and finds the corresponding location on the grid. For example, if Player 1 rolls C5, he locates the fifth square down in the C column.
4. Player 1 then proceeds to answer the question in the C5 square and records the answer on the student recording sheet. If he

answers the question correctly, he places a colored counter on the C5 square on the game board. If he does not answer correctly, Player 2 may answer the question and cover the square.

5. Player 2 then rolls the two cubes, finds the square indicated, and answers the question. As above, if Player 2 answers the question correctly, she covers it with a colored counter. If she misses it, Player 1 may answer the question.

6. Play continues until a player has a specified number of counters in a row, horizontally, vertically, or diagonally, or has covered the entire grid if that was the goal.

7. If a player rolls the cubes and the square has already been covered, the player will roll again.

Common Core State Standards for Mathematics Addressed

Apply and extend previous understandings of numbers to the system of rational numbers.

CCSS.Math.Content.6.NS.C.7 Understand ordering and absolute value of rational numbers.

CCSS.Math.Content.6.NS.C.7c Understand the absolute value of a rational number as its distance from 0 on the number line; interpret absolute value as magnitude for a positive or negative quantity in a real-world situation. *For example, for an account balance of −30 dollars, write* $|-30| = 30$ *to describe the size of the debt in dollars.*

Solve real-life and mathematical problems involving angle measure, area, surface area, and volume.

CCSS.Math.Content.7.G.B.4 Know the formulas for the area and circumference of a circle and use them to solve problems; give an informal derivation of the relationship between the circumference and area of a circle.

Work with radicals and integer exponents.

CCSS.Math.Content.8.EE.A.2 Use square root and cube root symbols to represent solutions to equations of the form $x^2 = p$ and $x^3 = p$, where p is a positive rational number. Evaluate square roots of small perfect squares and cube roots of small perfect cubes. Know that $\sqrt{2}$ is irrational.

(Common Core State Standards Initiative, 2012a)

Example: Circles

$$C = 2\pi r = \pi d \qquad A = \pi r^2$$

	A	B	C	D	E	F
Find the circumference and/or area of each circle with the given radius (r) or diameter (d).						
1	12	r = 3	20	18	r = 4	13
2	r = 2	22	19	r = 7	d = 6	12
3	28	d = 1	d = 9	r = 8	20	d = 12
4	r = 9	22	d = 8	12	d = 14	r = 5
5	d = 16	r = 1	18	14	d = 20	15
6	28	d = 1	40	d = 4	14	15

www.gridgamesgalore.com
A reproducible version of this tool is available in Appendix A (p. 108).

Example: Squares and Square Roots 2*

Solve each story problem involving square roots.

	A	B	C	D	E
1	A square has an area of 25 ft². What is the measure of each side?	$\sqrt{71}$ falls between which two whole numbers?	$\sqrt{150}$ falls between which two whole numbers?	A square picture has an area of 169 in². What is the measure of each side?	$\sqrt{50}$ falls between which two whole numbers?
2	$\sqrt{98}$ falls between which two whole numbers?	$\sqrt{150}$ is close to which whole number?	$\sqrt{15}$ falls between which two whole numbers?	$\sqrt{98}$ is close to which whole number?	A square has an area of 64 cm². What is the measure of each side?
3	$\sqrt{66}$ is close to which whole number?	A square has an area of 81 mm². What is the measure of each side?	$\sqrt{47}$ is close to which whole number?	$\sqrt{55}$ is close to which whole number?	$\sqrt{200}$ falls between which two whole numbers?
4	A square sign on the highway has an area of 196 ft². What is the measure of one side?	$\sqrt{70}$ falls between which two whole numbers?	A square card has an area of 144 cm². What is the measure of each side?	$\sqrt{30}$ falls between which two whole numbers?	A square poster has an area of 225 cm². What is the measure of each side?
5	$\sqrt{111}$ falls between which two whole numbers?	$\sqrt{10}$ is close to which whole number?	$\sqrt{180}$ falls between which two whole numbers?	A square paper has an area of 49 in². What is the measure of one side?	$\sqrt{40}$ is close to which whole number?

www.gridgamesgalore.com

A reproducible version of this tool is available in Appendix A (p. 111).

*Grid Games Galore (www.gridgamesgalore.com) features two versions of this activity. This is the second.

Example: Absolute Value

	A	B	C	D	E	F
			Simplify each expression below.			
1	$\lvert 3 - 2\rvert + 5$ when x = 6	$3\lvert 9 - 38\rvert$	$-2\lvert 51 - 74\rvert$	$\lvert 16 - 21\rvert - 41$	$12 - \lvert x + 10\rvert$ when x = −2	$\lvert 8 - 3x\rvert$ when x = −5
2	$-2\lvert 11 - 28\rvert$	$5 + \lvert x - 14\rvert$ when x = −8	$8 - \lvert 14 - 3x\rvert$ when x = −5	$11 + \lvert x + 6\rvert$ when x = −5	$-\lvert 5 - 19\rvert + 4$	$-\lvert 51 - 39\rvert$
3	$\lvert 5 - 2x\rvert - 5$ when x = 3	$-2\lvert 2 - 27\rvert$	$5 + \lvert 4 - 6x\rvert$ when x=5	$\frac{1}{2}\lvert 49 - 31\rvert$	$-\frac{1}{2}\lvert 12 + (-34)$	$\lvert 13 - x\rvert + 4$ when x = −4
4	$-2\lvert -14 - 21\rvert$	$7 - \lvert 4x + 9\rvert$ when x = −1	$\lvert 32 - (-23)\rvert$	$12 - \lvert x - 4\rvert$ when x = 8	$\lvert 9 - 3x\rvert - 6$ when x = 4	$\lvert -14 - 37\rvert$
5	$12 - \lvert x - 11\rvert$ when x = 8	$-\frac{1}{3}\lvert -12 + 42\rvert$	$\frac{3}{5}\lvert 8-63\rvert$	$\lvert 2x + 3\rvert + 1$ when x = 6	$3 - \lvert x - 4\rvert$ when x = 9	$-3\lvert -7 + (-18)\rvert$
6	$-\lvert 10 - 21\rvert - 8$	$\lvert 5 + 2x\rvert + 11$ when x = −4	$12 - \lvert x - 11\rvert$ when x = 8	$-\frac{1}{2}\lvert 8 - 43\rvert$	$\lvert -8 - 12\rvert - 17$	$\lvert 12 - x\rvert - 4$ when x = −7

Guided Facilitation

Grid Games serve as nice formative assessments. These games can be modified, through questioning, to support the standards indicated or serve as a pre-assessment option for review. Playing the games helps struggling students as well as students who need some review at any grade level.

1. To conserve resources, two grid games could be run off using the front and back of the cardstock. This also allows for differentiation.
2. Putting the grid games in sheet protectors and using two different colors of dry-erase markers eliminates the need for counters.
3. To eliminate the element of chance and to allow students to incorporate strategy, the cubes or spinners are not used. Instead, the students choose where they want to try to claim a cell.
4. If there is a discrepancy in answers, students must "construct a viable argument" or "critique the reasoning of others" to come to consensus.

Matching Mania

Overview

Matching Mania is a strategy that can be applied in multiple ways. As a pre-assessment tool, this strategy allows teachers to gauge where students are in their understanding of a particular topic or skill, their use of the associated vocabulary, and their development in the Standards for Mathematical Practice. Embedded in formative instruction, this strategy becomes a quick and easy transitional activity to check students' understanding of specific content or skills. Matching Mania can also be used as a tool to help students build fluencies. It could even be used as a nonthreatening way to engage students in intervention for skills in which they have gaps.

Students match the problems with the various answers and record on a sheet provided. Each activity is run off on cardstock and cut into pieces. Nothing else is needed. If the objective is to build fluency or check for fluency, give students both sets of cards. Have the students "create a viable argument" for at least five of the matches. Other students' arguments could also be shared and critiqued. To focus on problem solving, give the students only the problem cards. Have them determine the solutions, explain their strategy, and justify their reasoning. They then check their work using the answer cards provided. In cases where there are multiple matches to be made, it is best to initially give the students only one set of cards to match at a time. Later, multiple sets can be used as students' proficiency develops.

Matching Mania was developed by Melisa Rice and is being shared with permission. Additional card sets and topics can be found at www.gridgamesgalore.com.

Directions

1. All student recording sheets are numbered down the left side with the problem number correlating to the problem number found in the upper left corner of the problem cards.

2. Copy each set of cards within the activity on different colored paper or cardstock. This will allow students to easily differentiate the problem cards from the answer cards.
3. Matching Mania requires time in cutting out each activity. You might seek parent volunteers or perhaps student groups that can do this as part of community service hours, or you can have your students cut out the problems and solutions as they work.
4. There are several ways to organize the materials for efficient storage. Use zipper lock quart-size bags to store each set of Matching Mania activity cards. Use gallon bags to store all the individual activity cards, as well as extra recording sheets and the answer key.

Common Core State Standards for Mathematics Addressed

Reason about and solve one-variable equations and inequalities.

CCSS.Math.Content.6.EE.B.5 Understand solving an equation or inequality as a process of answering a question: which values from a specified set, if any, make the equation or inequality true? Use substitution to determine whether a given number in a specified set makes an equation or inequality true.

CCSS.Math.Content.6.EE.B.8 Write an inequality of the form $x > c$ or $x < c$ to represent a constraint or condition in a real-world or mathematical problem. Recognize that inequalities of the form $x > c$ or $x < c$ have infinitely many solutions; represent solutions of such inequalities on number line diagrams.

Apply and extend previous understandings of numbers to the system of rational numbers.

CCSS.Math.Content.6.NS.C.5 Understand that positive and negative numbers are used together to describe quantities having opposite directions or values (e.g., temperature above/below zero, elevation above/below sea level, credits/debits, positive/negative electric charge); use positive and negative numbers to represent quantities in real-world contexts, explaining the meaning of 0 in each situation.

Solve real-life and mathematical problems using numerical and algebraic expressions and equations.

CCSS.Math.Content.7.EE.B.4 Use variables to represent quantities in a real-world or mathematical problem, and construct simple equations and inequalities to solve problems by reasoning about the quantities.

CCSS.Math.Content.7.EE.B.4b Solve word problems leading to inequalities of the form $px + q > r$ or $px + q < r$, where p, q, and r are specific rational numbers. Graph the solution set of the inequality and interpret it in the context of the problem. *For example: As a salesperson, you are paid $50 per week plus $3 per sale. This week you want your pay to be at least $100. Write an inequality for the number of sales you need to make, and describe the solutions.*

Apply and extend previous understandings of operations with fractions to add, subtract, multiply, and divide rational numbers.

CCSS.Math.Content.7.NS.A.1 Apply and extend previous understandings of addition and subtraction to add and subtract rational numbers; represent addition and subtraction on a horizontal or vertical number line diagram.

Define, evaluate, and compare functions.

CCSS.Math.Content.8.F.A.3 Interpret the equation $y = mx + b$ as defining a linear function, whose graph is a straight line; give examples of functions that are not linear. *For example, the function A = s2 giving the area of a square as a function of its side length is not linear because its graph contains the points (1,1), (2,4) and (3,9), which are not on a straight line.*

(Common Core State Standards Initiative, 2012a)

————■————

Example: Inequalities

1 0 1 2	**2** −5 −4 −3	**3** −10 −9 −8	**4** 5 6 7
8 −10 −9 −8	**7** 4 5 6	**6** −1 0 1	**5** 0 1 2
9 4 5 6	**10** 2 3 4	**11** −4 −3 −2	**12** −4 −3 −2
16 −3 −2 −1	**15** −8 −7 −6	**14** −14 −13 −12	**13** −4 −3 −2

A reproducible version of this tool is available in Appendix A (pp. 117–119).

i. $2x - 4 \leq -8$	**f.** $-x - 8 \geq -5$	**k.** $2x + 3 < 9$	**h.** $2x + 6 \geq -8$
n. $-3x \leq 9$	**c.** $-x - 5 \geq 8$	**m.** $-3x - 4 < 5$	**a.** $x + -4 \leq -3$
d. $4x - 2 < 0$	**o.** $4x \geq 24$	**b.** $-2x - 15 \leq 3$	**l.** $5x < 5$
e. $5 > x$	**p.** $3x \geq -12$	**g.** $9x + 7 \leq 8x - 2$	**j.** $-15 \leq -3x$

C. $x \leq 5$

J. $x < 5$

D. $x \geq -4$

N. $x \leq -9$

L. $x \leq 1$

I. $x \geq -9$

A. $x \leq -13$

H. $x > -3$

K. $x < 1$

M. $x < \dfrac{1}{2}$

G. $x \geq 6$

B. $x \geq -3$

P. $x \geq -7$

E. $x \leq -2$

F. $x \leq -3$

O. $x < 3$

www.gridgamesgalore.com

Inequalities Scorecard

Graph	Inequality	Solution	Translate to words
1			
2			
3			
4			
5			
6			
7			
8			
9			
10			
11			
12			
13			
14			
15			
16			

Example: Integer Operations

1 −11 9	**2** −10 14
3 14 −5	**4** 9 −16
5 21 −3	**6** −21 11
7 −15 −11	**8** 8 −20
9 −10 24	**10** −17 −3
11 −5 11	**12** −24 −19
13 1 −7	**14** −3 18
15 −21 −15	**16** 0 −15
17 −9 4	**18** −5 18

A. sum = −43	R. sum = 18
B. sum = −36	Q. sum = 15
C. sum = −26	P. sum = 14
D. sum = −20	O. sum = 13
E. sum = −15	N. sum = 9
F. sum = −12	M. sum = 6
G. sum = −10	L. sum = 4
H. sum = −7	K. sum = −2
I. sum = −6	J. sum = −5

A. difference = −34	**R.** difference = −32
B. difference = −24	**Q.** difference = −23
C. difference = −21	**P.** difference = −20
D. difference = −16	**O.** difference = −14
E. difference = −13	**N.** difference = −6
F. difference = −5	**M.** difference = −4
G. difference = 8	**L.** difference = 15
H. difference = 19	**K.** difference = 24
I. difference = 25	**J.** difference = 28

a. product = 456	r. product = 315
b. product = 165	q. product = 51
c. product = 0	p. product = −7
d. product = −36	o. product = −54
e. product = −55	n. product = −63
f. product = −70	m. product = −90
g. product = −99	l. product = −140
h. product = −144	k. product = −160
i. product = −231	j. product = −240

Integer Operations Scorecards

Integers	Sum	Difference	Product
1			
2			
3			
4			
5			
6			
7			
8			
9			
10			
11			
12			
13			
14			
15			
16			
17			
18			

Integers	Sum	Difference	Product
1			
2			
3			
4			
5			
6			
7			
8			
9			
10			
11			
12			
13			
14			
15			
16			
17			
18			

Example: Linear Functions

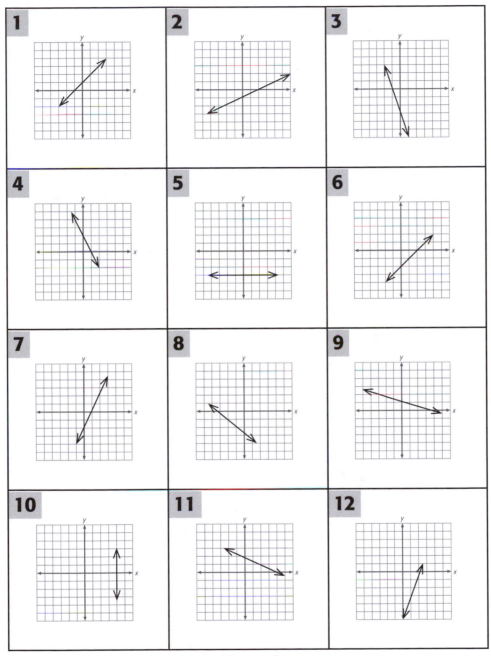

A reproducible version of this tool is available in Appendix A (pp. 128–130).

A. $y = -3x - 3$	B. $y = -2x + 2$
C. $y = \frac{1}{2}x - 1$	D. $y = 2x - 2$
E. $x = 4$	F. $y = x + 1$
G. $y = \frac{1}{2}x + 2$	H. $y = -x - 3$
I. $y = -\frac{1}{3} + 1$	J. $y = -3$
K. $y = x - 2$	L. $y = 3x - 6$

a.	b.
$m = -2$ $b = 2$	$m = 2$ $b = -2$

c.	d.
$m = \dfrac{1}{2}$ $b = 2$	$m = 1$ $b = 1$

e.	f.
$m = -1$ $b = -3$	$m = 0$ $b = -3$

g.	h.
$m = \dfrac{1}{2}$ $b = -1$	$m = \dfrac{1}{3}$ $b = 1$

i.	j.
$m = 1$ $b = -2$	$m = -3$ $b = -3$

k.	l.
$m = 3$ $b = -6$	m is undefined no b value

Linear Functions Scorecards

Graph	Slope Intercept Form	Slope and y-intercept
1		
2		
3		
4		
5		
6		
7		
8		
9		
10		
11		
12		

Graph	Slope Intercept Form	Slope and y-intercept
1		
2		
3		
4		
5		
6		
7		
8		
9		
10		
11		
12		

A reproducible version of this tool is available in Appendix A (p. 131).

Guided Facilitation

Inequalities

Teachers can use Inequalities Matching Mania as a pre-assessment strategy to gauge students' understanding of basic equations and inequalities, properties of operations, and associated vocabulary. Embedded in formative instruction, this strategy becomes a quick and easy transitional activity to check students' understanding of finding a solution to an inequality in one variable. Matching Mania can be used as a tool to help students build procedural fluency with solving basic inequalities and to support the development of related standards. It can also be used as a nonthreatening way to engage students in intervention for skills in which they have gaps.

♦ Inequalities Matching Mania consists of 16 inequalities graphed on a number line. Students identify the number line graphs by their inequality as well as the solution to the inequality. Students then complete the worksheet by translating to words the inequality given.

♦ The student recording sheet, graphs, and the appropriate forms of the answer are listed below:
  • Student recording sheet
  • The number line graphs of the inequalities
  • The inequalities
  • The solution to each inequality
  • Answer key

♦ Place students in pairs. Students work as pairs matching the appropriate solutions to each problem and filling out the recording sheet.

Integer Operations

Teachers can use Integer Operations Matching Mania as a pre-assessment strategy to gauge students' understanding of positive and negative numbers, operating with integers, and associated vocabulary. Embedded in formative instruction, this strategy becomes a quick and easy transitional activity to check students' understanding of operating with integers. Matching Mania can also be used as a tool to help students build procedural fluency in operating with integers. It can also be a nonthreatening way to engage students in intervention for skills in which they have gaps.

♦ Integer Operations Matching Mania consists of 18 pairs of integers on which the basic operations of addition, subtraction, and multiplication can be performed. Students will perform each operation to find the appropriate answer.

- ◆ The student recording sheet and the appropriate forms of the answer are listed below:
  - Student recording sheet
  - Integer pairs
  - Sum of the integer pairs
  - Difference of the integer pairs
  - Product of the integer pairs
  - Answer key
- ◆ Place students in pairs. Students work as pairs matching the appropriate solutions to each problem and filling out the recording sheet.

Linear Functions

Teachers can use Linear Functions Matching Mania as a pre-assessment strategy to gauge students' understanding of slope, y-intercept, graphing linear functions, and associated vocabulary. Embedded in formative instruction, this strategy becomes a quick and easy transitional activity to check students' understanding of slope-intercept form of a linear function and graphs of linear functions. Matching Mania can also be used as a tool to help students build confidence in graphing lines and using slope-intercept form. It can also be a nonthreatening way to engage students in intervention for skills in which they have gaps.

- ◆ Linear Functions Matching Mania consists of 12 linear graphs. The lines may then be identified by slope-intercept form and slope as well as y-intercept. Students may identify one or both concepts given the graphs.
- ◆ The student recording sheet, graphs, and the appropriate forms of the answer are listed below:
  - Student recording sheet
  - The graphs of the lines
  - The equations of the lines in slope-intercept form
  - The slope (m) and y-intercept (b) of each line
  - Answer key
- ◆ Place students in pairs. Students work as pairs matching the appropriate solutions to each problem and filling out the recording sheet.

Walk This Way

Overview

Walk This Way allows students to use repeated reasoning to investigate mathematical concepts on horizontal and/or vertical number lines as well as the Cartesian coordinate plane by physically representing mathematical situations on a life-size graph. Students walk an integer number line to represent quantities "having opposite directions or values" (CCSS.Math. Content.6.NS.C.5) as well as quantities "in real-world contexts, explaining the meaning of zero in each situation" (CCSS.Math.Content.6.NS.C.5). Students also analyze how the graphs of parent functions are transformed on the Cartesian coordinate plane. By asking probing questions rather than just repeating formulas and telling how each of the variables and coefficients affects the graph, students are better able to develop meaning on their own and understand how these functions behave.

> **NOTE:** The emphasis of this activity is transformations on the Cartesian coordinate plane and not the use of function notation.

Directions

1. Place students in groups of five (or four or six as needed).
2. Assign each student an x-coordinate with x values of $(-2, -1, 0, 1, 2)$.
3. Given x, the students evaluate the given transformation equations for y and record the results as an ordered pair. A linear example is given below.
   $y = x$
   $y = -x$
   $y = x + 3$
   $y = x - 3$
   $y = 3x$
   $y = \frac{1}{3}x$

NOTE: The transformation equations will change depending on the parent function used.

4. A large Cartesian coordinate plane will be needed so the students can physically graph their coordinates. This could be a painter's tarp that has been prepped, the tiles on the classroom floor with the x- and y-axes marked, or the football field with axes drawn. Prep by drawing a coordinate plane with D = {$-10 < x < 10$} and R = {$-10 < y < 10$}. Be sure to label the axes.

5. The first student group demonstrates how to physically graph the parent function with each student representing an ordered pair. Have all students draw what they see on the student recording sheet provided.

6. Discuss what the students observe. See examples of probing questions in the Guided Facilitation section. Students will describe what they see in terms of what the graph resembles. (They should describe this parent function as a line. Note that student vocabulary will reflect past mathematical experiences.)

7. The next student group will graph the next transformation equation and compare their graph to the graph of $y = x$ (or whatever parent function is being used). Discuss what component in the equation is responsible for the observed transformation. Continue this process for the remaining transformation equations on the student recording sheet.

Common Core State Standards for Mathematics Addressed

Apply and extend previous understandings of numbers to the system of rational numbers.

CCSS.Math.Content.6.NS.C.5 Understand that positive and negative numbers are used together to describe quantities having opposite directions or values (e.g., temperature above/below zero, elevation above/below sea level, credits/debits, positive/negative electric charge); use positive and negative numbers to represent quantities in real-world contexts, explaining the meaning of 0 in each situation.

CCSS.Math.Content.6.NS.C.6 Understand a rational number as a point on the number line. Extend number line diagrams and coordinate axes familiar from previous grades to represent points on the line and in the plane with negative number coordinates.

CCSS.Math.Content.6.NS.C.6a Recognize opposite signs of numbers as indicating locations on opposite sides of 0 on the number line; recognize that the opposite of the opposite of a number is the number itself, e.g., $-(-3) = 3$, and that 0 is its own opposite.

CCSS.Math.Content.6.NS.C.6b Understand signs of numbers in ordered pairs as indicating locations in quadrants of the coordinate plane; recognize that when two ordered pairs differ only by signs, the locations of the points are related by reflections across one or both axes.

CCSS.Math.Content.6.NS.C.6c Find and position integers and other rational numbers on a horizontal or vertical number line diagram; find and position pairs of integers and other rational numbers on a coordinate plane.

CCSS.Math.Content.6.NS.C.7 Understand ordering and absolute value of rational numbers.

CCSS.Math.Content.6.NS.C.7b Write, interpret, and explain statements of order for rational numbers in real-world contexts. *For example, write −3°C > −7°C to express the fact that −3°C is warmer than −7°C.*

CCSS.Math.Content.6.NS.C.7c Understand the absolute value of a rational number as its distance from 0 on the number line; interpret absolute value as magnitude for a positive or negative quantity in a real-world situation. *For example, for an account balance of −30 dollars, write $|-30| = 30$ to describe the size of the debt in dollars.*

CCSS.Math.Content.6.NS.C.7d Distinguish comparisons of absolute value from statements about order. *For example, recognize that an account balance less than −30 dollars represents a debt greater than 30 dollars.*

CCSS.Math.Content.6.NS.C.8 Solve real-world and mathematical problems by graphing points in all four quadrants of the coordinate plane. Include use of coordinates and absolute value to find distances between points with the same first coordinate or the same second coordinate.

Apply and extend previous understandings of operations with fractions.

CCSS.Math.Content.7.NS.A.1 Apply and extend previous understandings of addition and subtraction to add and subtract rational numbers; represent addition and subtraction on a horizontal or vertical number line diagram.

CCSS.Math.Content.7.NS.A.1a Describe situations in which opposite quantities combine to make 0. *For example, a hydrogen atom has 0 charge because its two constituents are oppositely charged.*

CCSS.Math.Content.7.NS.A.1b Understand $p + q$ as the number located a distance $|q|$ from p, in the positive or negative direction depending on whether q is positive or negative. Show that a number and its opposite have a sum of 0 (are additive inverses). Interpret sums of rational numbers by describing real-world contexts.

CCSS.Math.Content.7.NS.A.1c Understand subtraction of rational numbers as adding the additive inverse, $p − q = p + (−q)$. Show that the distance between two rational numbers on the number line is the absolute value of their difference, and apply this principle in real-world contexts.

Define, evaluate, and compare functions.

CCSS.Math.Content.8.F.A.1 Understand that a function is a rule that assigns to each input exactly one output. The graph of a function is the set of ordered pairs consisting of an input and the corresponding output.

CCSS.Math.Content.8.F.A.2 Compare properties of two functions each represented in a different way (algebraically, graphically, numerically in tables, or by verbal descriptions). *For example, given a linear function represented by a table of values and a linear function represented by an algebraic expression, determine which function has the greater rate of change.*

CCSS.Math.Content.8.F.A.3 Interpret the equation $y = mx + b$ as defining a linear function, whose graph is a straight line; give examples of functions that are not linear. *For example, the function $A = s^2$ giving the area of a square as a function of its side length is not linear because its graph contains the points (1,1), (2,4) and (3,9), which are not on a straight line.*

Use functions to model relationships between quantities.

CCSS.Math.Content.8.F.B.5 Describe qualitatively the functional relationship between two quantities by analyzing a graph (e.g., where the function is increasing or decreasing, linear or nonlinear). Sketch a graph that exhibits the qualitative features of a function that has been described verbally.

(Common Core State Standards Initiative, 2012a)

———————■———————

Example: Linear Equations

Assigned x-coordinate _____

Solve the following equations for y and then write as an ordered pair:

$y = x$ **Ordered pair (** _____ **,** _____ **) (Parent Function)**
$y = -x$ Ordered pair (_____ , _____)
$y = x + 3$ Ordered pair (_____ , _____)
$y = x - 3$ Ordered pair (_____ , _____)
$y = 3x$ Ordered pair (_____ , _____)
$y = \frac{1}{3}x$ Ordered pair (_____ , _____)

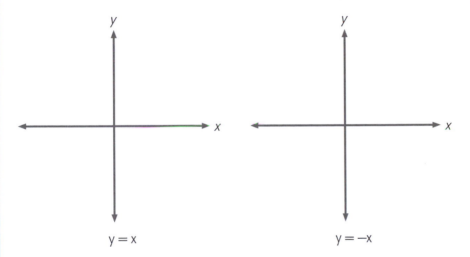

Compare the graph of y = x and y = -x. What do you notice about the difference in the look of the two graphs? Discuss what component in the equation is responsible for the observed transformation.

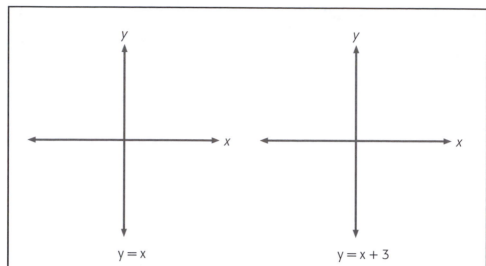

$$y = x \qquad\qquad y = x + 3$$

Compare the graph of y = x and y = x + 3. What do you notice about the difference in the look of the two graphs? Discuss what component in the equation is responsible for the observed transformation.

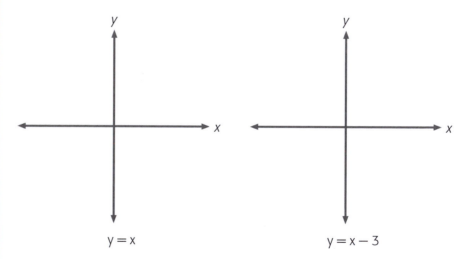

$$y = x \qquad\qquad y = x - 3$$

Compare the graph of y = x and y = x − 3. What do you notice about the difference in the look of the two graphs? Discuss what component in the equation is responsible for the observed transformation.

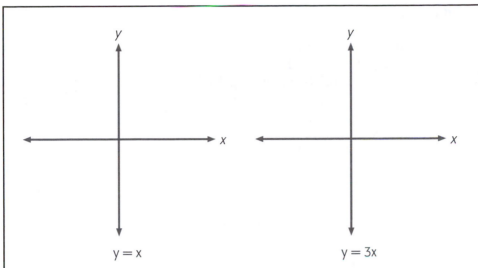

$$y = x \qquad\qquad y = 3x$$

Compare the graph of y = x and y = 3x. What do you notice about the difference in the look of the two graphs? Discuss what component in the equation is responsible for the observed transformation.

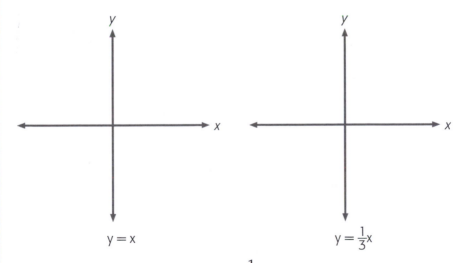

$$y = x \qquad\qquad y = \tfrac{1}{3}x$$

Compare the graph of y = x and y = $\frac{1}{3}$x. What do you notice about the difference in the look of the two graphs? Discuss what component in the equation is responsible for the observed transformation.

What do you think the graph of y = −3x + 1 will look like? Explain your reasoning.

A reproducible version of this tool is available in Appendix A (pp. 133–135).

Guided Facilitation

Begin with the parent function $y = x$. Have the members of the first student group begin by standing on the x coordinate of the ordered pair to which they were assigned. From here, have each student walk to the corresponding y coordinate to complete the ordered pair. Have the group members hold colored yarn (or anything comparable) to illustrate the fact that these points are connected in a line. Have all students sketch what they observe from the student model on the student recording sheet provided.

 NOTE: The emphasis is on sketching what they see and not plotting points and connecting the dots. This is the reason for providing only an x and y axis on the student recording sheet rather than a coordinate grid.

Discuss what students observe. Students will describe what they see in terms of what the graph resembles (a line). Additional student observations might include the following:

♦ The line is rising to the right of the vertical. (At this point, students may not have prior knowledge of slope and might not be able to describe the line as increasing or decreasing.)
♦ The line is diagonal and cuts the first and third quadrants in half.
♦ The line crosses the origin.

Let students know this will be the parent function to which all other graphs will be compared. All student groups will begin from this parent function and will move to the next equation to facilitate visualizing the transformations. For example, group 2 will begin by standing on the $y = x$ line and then move to the next ordered pair found when they solved $y = -x$. Have all students sketch what they see on the sheet provided. Discuss what students observe. Students will describe what they see in terms of what the graph resembles (a line). Additional student observations might include the following:

♦ The line is facing to the left of the vertical.
♦ The line is diagonal and cuts the second and fourth quadrants in half.
♦ The line seems to be the same slope as the line $y = x$.
♦ The line crosses the origin.

Ask the students to consider how the graph of this line compares to the original parent function. Responses will point out that the direction of the line has changed. Discuss what component in the equation is responsible for the observed transformation. Students will state that the sign in front of the x has changed from positive to negative, thus causing the directional change in the graph. This is a good time to connect the fact that "negative" is also referred to as "the opposite of" so it would make sense that the graph would be facing in the opposite direction.

NOTE: As an extension, students can see that the line was reflected over the **y**-axis.

Continue the process for the remaining equations, always beginning with the parent function, and discussing each transformation as it relates to the equation. (See student recording sheet.)

Once the activity has been completed, ask students to describe the graph of $y = -3x + 1$. Have them explain their reasoning. Students should describe what they learned about transformations from the activity. A typical response might be that the graph will be facing to the left (because of the negative), it will move up one space on the y-axis (because of the +1), and it will be "steeper," or closer to the y-axis, than $y = x$ (because of the coefficient of 3).

Continue the discussion with additional linear equations and have students describe and sketch each. Be careful to ask students to provide reasons for the descriptions. From here, questioning can begin to lead students to formalize the relationships they now understand. For example, students will typically refer to the slope of the graph and that the larger the coefficient of x, the steeper the line becomes; the smaller the coefficient, the less steep the line becomes. Monitor that the students are using proper vocabulary.

The same connection can be made with respect to the y-intercept. Students will have been referring to whether the line has shifted up or down. Ask students to consider what else they notice about the graph as it shifted. If no one sees that it also indicates where the line crosses the y-axis, you may want to circle that point on one of the examples you have previously graphed. Once students see that this point is where the line crosses the y-axis, be sure they note that the point $(0, y)$ is the y-intercept. This is one of the points of interest in analyzing linear graphs. As students continue their study of functions, they will note other points of interest. By explicitly referring to these points of interest, students begin to develop efficiency in identifying the key features of graphs through reasoning from their repeated observations.

Next, ask the students, "If given the slope and the y-intercept, but not the actual equation of the line, can you sketch the graph?" For example, if the slope is 4 and the y-intercept is –2, sketch the graph of the line they determine. Have students sketch the graph and then ask them to see if they can write the equation of the line. Discuss.

From here, reinforce the fact that students have now demonstrated they can sketch the graph of the line given only the slope and the y-intercept.

Refer to the equation and point out that based on that fact, $y =$ (slope) $x + y$-intercept or $y =$ _?_ $x +$ _?_ , where we can substitute any number into the blanks and have the equation of the line. Ask students what we use to represent the missing values. Consequently, we will represent the slope with the letter m and the y-intercept with the letter b. Using substitution, we now have $y = mx + b$ to represent the slope-intercept form of the equation of a line.

Extensions

In addition to investigating transformations on a parent function on the Cartesian coordinate plane, Walk This Way can be adapted for investigating the concepts of positive and negative quantities. For example, a vertical number line can represent a thermometer with "degrees below zero" modeled with the negative integers. The same idea can be used for above and below sea level. Operations with integers can also be investigated on the horizontal number line as well as graphing inequalities in one variable.

What's My Move?

Overview

This activity is adapted from universal problems such as Traffic Jam or Tower of Hanoi. The basic setup below shows two people on each side of the table with an empty space on one end and a "dead end" on the other. The objective is to move all the players from one side of the table to the other side and vice versa in the fewest moves possible.

Embedded in this one activity are most all the Standards for Mathematical Practice. Students are engaged in a task that requires them to reason to find solutions to the problem posed. They have to justify their findings while using precise mathematical language, symbols, and notation. The students while investigating this task can employ a variety of tools. Through discerning various possible patterns, students are asked to develop a mathematical model to describe the physical movements of the participants.

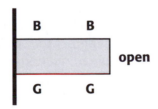

Directions

1. Only one player may move at a time.
2. A player may only "slide" (move) into an open space.
3. Players must continue moving in the same direction they began.
4. A player may only "jump" (go around) a player from the other team. For example, in the diagram above, a B can only jump around a G and vice versa.

NOTE: If there are no viable moves, the players must start over. Many groups will try to "undo" moves rather than restarting the activity. This is not allowed.

Common Core State Standards for Mathematics Addressed

CCSS.Math.Content.6.EE.A.2 Write, read, and evaluate expressions in which letters stand for numbers.

> CCSS.Math.Content.6.EE.A.2a Write expressions that record operations with numbers and with letters standing for numbers. *For example, express the calculation "Subtract y from 5" as $5 - y$.*

> CCSS.Math.Content.6.EE.A.2b Identify parts of an expression using mathematical terms (sum, term, product, factor, quotient, coefficient); view one or more parts of an expression as a single entity. *For example, describe the expression $2(8 + 7)$ as a product of two factors; view $(8 + 7)$ as both a single entity and a sum of two terms.*

> CCSS.Math.Content.6.EE.A.2c Evaluate expressions at specific values of their variables. Include expressions that arise from formulas used in real-world problems. Perform arithmetic operations, including those involving whole-number exponents, in the conventional order when there are no parentheses to specify a particular order (Order of Operations). *For example, use the formulas $V = s^3$ and $A = 6s^2$ to find the volume and surface area of a cube with sides of length $s = \frac{1}{2}$.*

CCSS.Math.Content.6.EE.B.5 Understand solving an equation or inequality as a process of answering a question: which values from a specified set, if any, make the equation or inequality true? Use substitution to determine whether a given number in a specified set makes an equation or inequality true.

CCSS.Math.Content.6.EE.B.6 Use variables to represent numbers and write expressions when solving a real-world or mathematical problem; understand that a variable can represent an unknown number, or, depending on the purpose at hand, any number in a specified set.

CCSS.Math.Content.6.EE.C.9 Use variables to represent two quantities in a real-world problem that change in relationship to one another; write an equation to express one quantity, thought of as the dependent variable, in terms of the other quantity, thought of as the independent variable. Analyze the relationship between the dependent and independent variables using graphs and tables, and relate these to the equation. *For example, in a problem involving motion at constant speed, list and graph ordered pairs of distances and times, and write the equation $d = 65t$ to represent the relationship between distance and time.*

CCSS.Math.Content.7.RP.A.2 Recognize and represent proportional relationships between quantities.

> CCSS.Math.Content.7.RP.A.2a Decide whether two quantities are in a proportional relationship, e.g., by testing for equivalent ratios in a table or graphing on a coordinate plane and observing whether the graph is a straight line through the origin.

CCSS.Math.Content.7.EE.B.4 Use variables to represent quantities in a real-world or mathematical problem, and construct simple equations and inequalities to solve problems by reasoning about the quantities.
CCSS.Math.Content.7.EE.B.4a Solve word problems leading to equations of the form $px + q = r$ and $p(x + q) = r$, where p, q, and r are specific rational numbers. Solve equations of these forms fluently. Compare an algebraic solution to an arithmetic solution, identifying the sequence of the operations used in each approach. *For example, the perimeter of a rectangle is 54 cm. Its length is 6 cm. What is its width?*
CCSS.Math.Content.8.F.A.3 Interpret the equation $y = mx + b$ as defining a linear function, whose graph is a straight line; give examples of functions that are not linear. *For example, the function $A = s^2$ giving the area of a square as a function of its side length is not linear because its graph contains the points (1,1), (2,4) and (3,9), which are not on a straight line.*
CCSS.Math.Content.8.F.B.5 Describe qualitatively the functional relationship between two quantities by analyzing a graph (e.g., where the function is increasing or decreasing, linear or nonlinear). Sketch a graph that exhibits the qualitative features of a function that has been described verbally.

(Common Core State Standards Initiative, 2012a)

Guided Facilitation

Begin with a demonstration group of four students. Choosing two boys and two girls makes it easier to distinguish which players began on the same side and allows students to keep track of the direction the players are moving. Allow the players to work together to complete the activity. The class may provide hints for the players if they are having trouble.

Once the demonstration group has successfully completed the exercise with 8 moves, have the players repeat the activity while the rest of the class records the movements, looking for patterns. You can have part of the class record "boy" (B) versus "girl" (G) moves and the remaining part of the class record "slides" (S) versus "jumps" (J) to get the patterns below.

B G G B B G G B

S J S J J S J S

NOTE: It is not necessary to differentiate between B_1, B_2, G_1, and G_2.

Begin with the first pattern and discuss what observations students have about the pattern. Various answers include, but are not limited to the following:

1. The pattern begins with a boy (B) and ends with a boy (B).
   NOTE: The same would be true if the exercise had begun with a girl.
2. There seems to be a repeated pattern of BGGB and then BGGB.
3. After the initial move, there are consecutive team moves: B GG BB GG B.
4. There are 4 boy (B) moves and 4 girl (G) moves.
5. The pattern is a palindrome.

Next, have students discuss the second pattern of slides (S) and jumps (J). Various answers include, but are not limited to the following:

1. The pattern begins with a slide (S) and ends with a slide (S).
2. There seems to be a reflexive pattern of SJSJ and then JSJS.
3. There are 4 slides (S) and 4 jumps (J).
4. The pattern is a palindrome.
5. There is a pattern in which the number of jumps (J) increases and then decreases between slides (S).

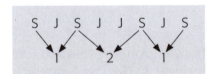

Let students know that these patterns may provide useful clues as the exercise continues.

Transition by asking students the following question: "Given the patterns above and knowing that with four people it took 8 moves, how many moves do you predict it would take for six people? Upon what criteria are you basing your answer?" Typically, students respond with such answers as 10 (adding 4 to the number of people), 12 (multiplying the number of people by 2), or 18 (multiplying the number of people by 3).

NOTE: If students ask at this point why the game uses only an even number of people, ask them to hold that question. It will be addressed as an extension exercise.

Assign students to groups of six, ensuring there is some visual cue that distinguishes students on one side of the table from the other (boy-girl, glasses-no glasses, shirt colors, etc). If there are no distinguishing charac-teristics, you can place colored sticky notes on students' shirts. Explain that students will check their predictions by completing the exercise with six people and recording the number of moves. *The answer is 15 moves.*

Ask students to repeat this exercise, but this time record the slide-jump sequence.

NOTE: The slide-jump pattern will be the focused pattern for the exercise. The boy-girl pattern can be used as an extension question.

Once finished, have students determine how many moves it would take with eight people and describe the method used for solving. You can use various methods, such as the following:

1. Complete the exercise physically with eight people.
2. Use manipulatives, such as colored chips, to simulate the movements.
3. Continue the S-J pattern on paper and then count the number of moves.

4. Develop a table and look for a numeric pattern; some students may recognize they could get additional data by doing the exercise with two people.

# of people (P)	# of moves (M)
4	8
6	15
8	?

+ 7

Define the variables:
P = number of people
M = number of moves
S = number of slides
J = number of jumps

Many students incorrectly believe the answer is 22 because they assume the pattern they are seeing is linear and the number of moves is increasing constantly by 7. Encourage them to use other methods or find additional data (without telling them to use two students, ask questions to allow them to realize this).

Another pattern can be seen between the number of people and the number of moves.

# of people (P)		# of moves (M)
4	multiplied by 2 =	8
6	multiplied by 2.5 =	15
8	multiplied by 3 =	?

Once an *answer of 24* moves has been reached, ask students to individually consider the number of moves it would take for ten people. This will assess whether all students have recognized a pattern and are able to use the pattern for additional situations.

NOTE: At this point, students will typically notice that the number of moves is increasing by consecutive odd integers.

Next, ask students to determine how many moves would be needed for 100 people. Asking for a specific number, rather than for students to "find the general rule," allows students the opportunity to answer the question from a variety of approaches. Since students are not familiar with quadratics at this point, they would be unable to write an equation, but they can still find the solution using other strategies. The goal of this question is not to teach how to create a quadratic equation, but rather to focus on the analysis of the patterns and the problem-solving strategies it affords.

The same methods used for determining the number of moves for eight people can be continued; however, some are not conducive to arriving at the answer in an efficient and timely manner. For example, it is not feasible to physically arrange 100 people to complete the activity. The same could be said for using manipulatives. Completing the table by adding consecutive odd integers would take considerable time and space, as would the strategy of continuing with the S-J pattern.

However, there are aspects of these methods that could be used to help students identify additional patterns. For example, students could expand the table to look for relationships between the types of movements.

Below are some prompts that can be used to promote student thinking about this question:

♦ How might creating a table of values help in answering the question?
♦ What are some ways of approaching the problem, such as were used to find the number of moves for eight or ten people?
♦ Are there any relationships between the variables (number of people; number of moves, slides, and jumps)? How will knowing these relationships help you address the question?

NOTE: You may want to assign groups of students to explore the various relationships, report their findings, and discuss as a group. Examples of relationships include:
- Number of moves and number of jumps (table shown earlier)
- Number of people and number of slides
- Number of jumps (perfect squares)
- Number of slides and number of jumps

Below are tables with examples of the relationships students will explore:

1. The number of people (P) = the number of slides (S)

# of people (P)	# of slides (S)	# of jumps (J)	# of moves (M)
4	4	$4 = 2^2$	8
6	6	$9 = 3^2$	15
8	8	$16 = 4^2$	24

2. The number of jumps (J) is a perfect square.

# of people (P)	# of slides (S)	# of jumps (J)	# of moves (M)
4	4	$4 = 2^2$	8
6	6	$9 = 3^2$	15
8	8	$16 = 4^2$	24

3. The number of jumps = (½ the number of slides)².
   NOTE: Since the number of slides = the number of people, we can conclude that the number of jumps = (½ the number of people)².

# of slides (S) = # of people (P)	$(½P)^2$	# of jumps (J)
4	½(4) = 2 $2^2 = 4$	4
6	½(6) = 3 $3^2 = 9$	9
8	½(8) = 4 $4^2 = 16$	16

Students can conclude that the total number of moves is equivalent to the sum of the number of slides and the number of jumps.

# of moves = # of slides + # of jumps
$$M = S + J$$
# of moves = # of people + (½ # of people)²

Using substitution, for 100 people

$$M = 100 + [½(100)]^2$$
$$M = 100 + (50)^2$$
$$M = 100 + 2500$$
$$M = 2600 \text{ moves}$$

Notice how students were able to follow this process to find a solution of 2,600 moves and did not need a formula.

Extension

From here, students can be led to substitute variables into the process to generalize for any number of people.

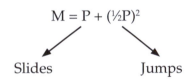

We already know
P = number of people
M = number of moves

# of moves = # of people + (½ # of people)²

$$M = P + (½P)^2$$

Slides   Jumps

It is important for students to understand the relationship between the equation and the physical movements from the exercise. Students need to understand that equations are developed in order to explain physical quantities and their relationship to one another. By using a real scenario and collecting actual data, students are better able to see the relationships and determine the mathematical connection.

Graphing the Results

Have students graph the data from the table (number of moves vs. number of people).

1. What should be the title of the graph?
2. What are the variables from the activity?
3. Which of the variables is independent? Which is dependent?
4. Which variable gets graphed on the x-axis? Which gets graphed on the y-axis?
5. How should the axes be labeled?

6. What is the domain and range?
7. What should be the interval on each axis?
8. Why do we only graph in the first quadrant?
9. What do we notice about the shape of the graph?
10. What predictions can we make from the graph? Do they follow from what we know is the number of moves for 100 people?

Once graphed, identify an ordered pair and ask students to explain what that ordered pair represents. For example, (10, 35) indicates that for 10 people, there would be 35 moves. Additional questions can be asked, such as the following: Is (25, 100) true for this activity?

An additional relationship that can be explored is looking at the number of people as pairs of people.

The following table compares the number of pairs of people (PP) to the number of jumps (J):

# of people (P)	# of pairs of people (PP)	$(PP)^2$	#of jumps (J)
4	2	$2^2 = 4$	4
6	3	$3^2 = 9$	9
8	4	$4^2 = 16$	13

Key Vocabulary and Concept Development
◆ Domain and range
◆ Independent vs. dependent variable
◆ Linear vs. nonlinear
◆ Reflexive
◆ Palindrome
◆ Integer

Appendix A

Five-Step Problem-Solving Process

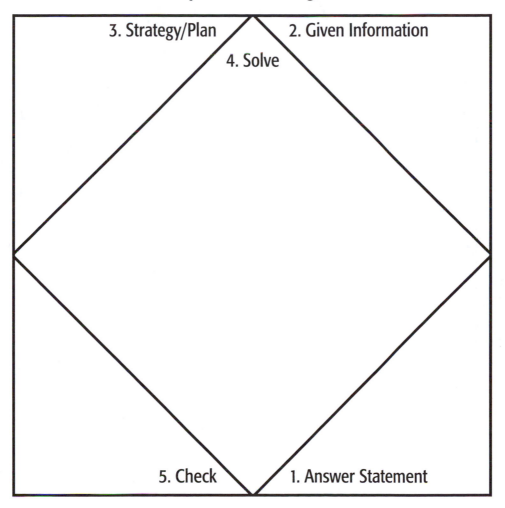

3. Strategy/Plan

2. Given Information

4. Solve

5. Check

1. Answer Statement

Five-Step Problem-Solving Process

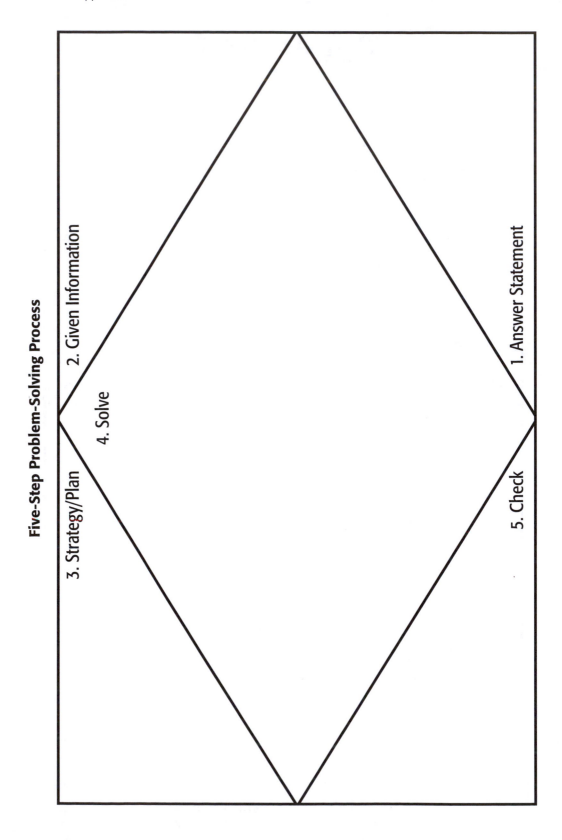

1. Answer Statement

2. Given Information

3. Strategy/Plan

4. Solve

5. Check

Visual Vocabulary Concept Mapping

Characteristics	Definition
Counterexample	Example

Puzzling Problems: Grade 6

Dave was shown the following data set:

92, 73, 86, 99, 85, 75

Determine the three measures of central tendency for this data set and explain their meaning with reference to the data set.

Looking at Dave's data set, list at least two real-life contexts in which these numbers could exist. Explain each of the measures of central tendency in context.

What would happen to each measure of central tendency if another number, 60, were added to the set? Explain your reasoning.

Thinking about what each of the measures of central tendency describes, list three numbers that could be added to the data set so:

a. the median does not change
b. the mean does not change
c. the mode does not change

Explain fully why there is no change in each of the three measures. Describe numbers that would change the three measures and explain why.

Puzzling Problems: Grade 7

Jamal used a spinner file he had on his handheld. The spinner is shown below.

Trials: 0

What is the probability of the spinner landing on each of the colored sections? Explain your thinking. Are there any values that could not be used to represent the probabilities? Why or why not?

Draw a circle graph showing what you predict the outcome would be for 10 spins.

Jamal set the program to spin the spinner 10 times. His results are shown in the picture on the right.

Trials: 10

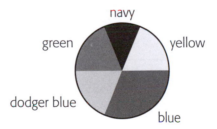

Results

How do these results compare to yours? Write a couple of statements about the differences and the reasons for these differences. Why were not all 8 colors shown?

Write a statement about what you think the results would look like for 100 spins, and explain your reasoning.

Jamal did set the program to spin 100 times.

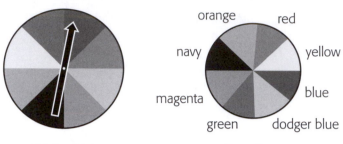

Trials: 100   **Results**

How do these results compare to yours? Write a couple of statements about the differences and the reasons for these differences. If you ran the simulation, how do you think your results would compare with Jamal's? Why?

Write a statement about what you think the results would look like for 1,000 spins, and explain your reasoning.

Is there a number of trials you could set the simulation for so the results would always be the same? Why or why not?

Puzzling Problems: Grade 8

Students in a middle-school class measured 10 circular objects and recorded their measurements below.

Object #	Circumference	Diameter
1	25 inches	$7\frac{1}{2}$ inches
2	8 inches	$2\frac{1}{2}$ inches
3	$4\frac{1}{2}$ inches	$1\frac{1}{2}$ inches
4	13 inches	4 inches
5	22 inches	$6\frac{1}{2}$ inches
6	68 inches	22 inches
7	14 inches	$4\frac{1}{2}$ inches
8	11 inches	$3\frac{1}{2}$ inches
9	$28\frac{1}{2}$ inches	9 inches
10	47 inches	15 inches

Create a scatter plot of the data. Discuss your observations about the scatter plot. Be specific.

Using the scatterplot created in part 1, fit a line to the scatterplot and assess the fit. Justify your reasoning. Identify the key features of the line used in your model. Discuss the relationship between the key features in the model and how those features relate to the context of the data.

What key feature of the model relates the circumference of a circle to its diameter?

How close was the students' collected data to the actual accepted model for the circumference of a circle?

Why do you think there was a difference?

Would it have mattered if the measurements had been in metric units?

What is the relationship between the area of a circle and the circle's diameter?

Puzzling Problems Answer Keys

6th Grade

The mean is 85, the median is 85.5, and this data set is amodal (meaning there is no mode).

The median is the center of location. So 85.5 is the center of the data ordered numerically from smallest to greatest. Since there is an even number of pieces of data, the median is the average of the third and fourth pieces of data. There is no mode. The mean can be understood as a fair share between the pieces of data. It is the measure that would be the equal part if the data were divided evenly between each of the six contributing samples.

Student answers will vary. Answers might include test grades, outside temperatures, ages of residents in a senior citizens' home, etc. Then the students need to relate the measures to their chosen context.

The new mean will become lower, 81.4, since the piece of data added was a smaller number. The median will also drop, 85, since now there is an odd number of pieces of data. The number 85 is the middle piece of data by location once the data are placed in numerical order. There is still no mode since 60 was not already a piece of data in the set.

For the third part, in order for the median not to change, students must add a number to the left of 85, add a number to the right of 86, and include 85.5. Otherwise, since there will now be nine pieces of data, the middle piece, by location, would be a whole number. For the mean not to change, the three numbers chosen must themselves have an average of 85 so when the total is added to the six pieces of original data and then divided by nine to calculate the new mean, it will still be 85. Any three numbers that are not already part of the data set can be introduced and not change the fact that there is no mode.

7th Grade

Part 1: Since there are eight equal sections on the spinner, the theoretical probability of landing on each section would be ⅛. A probability can only be $0 \leq p \leq 1$. So any number not contained within that set of numbers could not be used to represent a probability. Student graphs will vary.

Part 2: Student answers for the comparisons between their graphs and Jamal's will vary. Monitor their answers closely to check for any misconceptions in students' understanding of probability, especially the difference between theoretical and experimental probability—for example, why only five colors came up in the simulation, not all eight.

Student statements about what they predict for 100 will vary. Monitor their explanations closely.

Part 3: Student answers for the comparisons between their graphs and Jamal's will vary. Monitor their answers closely to check for any misconceptions in students' understanding of probability. They should begin to understand that the more times you run the simulation or perform the experiment, the closer you should come to the theoretical probability.

Student statements about what they predict for 1,000 will vary. Monitor their explanations closely.

There does not exist a number of trials, experiments, or simulations that would guarantee results matching the theoretical probability.

8th Grade

Students' scatter plots should resemble the plot below:

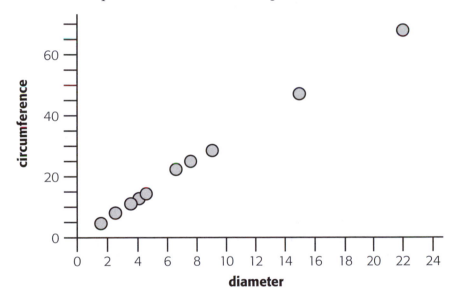

Student discussions should include comments about a strong positive correlation and a strong linear correlation.

Student lines of fit should be close to the line shown on the next page. The slope of the line approaches pi. Students should realize that the slope is pi and the intercept is close to zero, since this data models the function for the circumference of a circle in terms of its diameter.

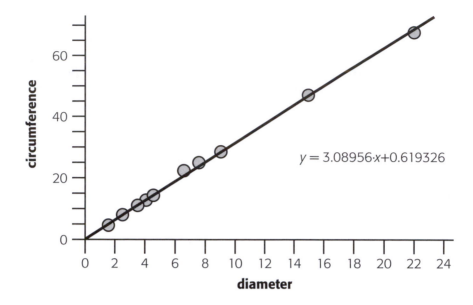

$$y = 3.08956 \cdot x + 0.619326$$

Students may have commented in the second part about the slope of the line being pi and the y-intercept being zero, since this is a direct variation and pi is the constant of proportionality. Monitor students' explanation for how close the data was to the actual value of pi. The difference might have been due to human error in measuring or in the choice of measuring devices. Remind students that a measurement can only be as precise as the measuring device. It would make no difference if metric units had been used, since pi is a ratio.

Students have used the formula for the area of a circle. The area of a circle is a function of the circle's radius, not the diameter, as is asked in the question. This question pushes students to begin to solve a basic literal equation for a certain variable, in this case r. Once that has been accomplished, students should see that the diameter of the circle is equivalent to twice the square root of the quotient of the area of the circle and pi. The algebra is shown below. Due to the context of the problem, only the principal square root is used.

$$A = \pi r^2$$
$$\frac{A}{\pi} = r^2$$
$$\sqrt{\frac{A}{\pi}} = r$$
$$2\sqrt{\frac{A}{\pi}} = 2r$$
$$2\sqrt{\frac{A}{\pi}} = d$$

ABC Sum Race Sample Cards

A. $8 + (2 \cdot 5) \times 3^4 \div 9$

B. $2^2 \cdot 20 \div 4 - 7 \cdot 3 + 55$

C. $4 - 3 [4 - 2 (6 - 3)] \div 2$

Solve for x.

A. $-2 (x - 3) - 4x = -8 + x$

B. $2x - 5 (x + 1) = 3x + 1$

C. $4x + 3 (2x - 4) = x$

Caleb has 11 red marbles, 15 green marbles, 8 yellow marbles, 5 white marbles, 9 blue marbles, and 2 black marbles in a bag. There are no other marbles in the bag.

A. What is the probability that Caleb will select at random either a red or black marble?
B. What is the probability that Caleb will select at random either a yellow or white marble?
C. What is the probability that Caleb will select at random either a green or blue marble?

Determine whether or not the triangle is a right triangle. Use the length of the hypotenuse, if it exists, as the number to create the sum. If the triangle is not a right triangle, use 0 as the number to sum.

A.   14, 48, 50

B.   12, 16, 25

C.   11, 60, 61

A.   Draw a net for a cube. How many faces does it have?

B.   A cube has a side of length 2.4 cm. Determine the surface area of the cube.

C.   A cube has a side of length 2.4 cm. Determine the volume of the cube.

ABC Sum Race Scorecards

	A	B	C	SUM
1				
2				
3				
4				
5				

	A	B	C	SUM
1				
2				
3				
4				
5				

	A	B	C	SUM
1				
2				
3				
4				
5				

ABC Sum Race Answer Key

	A	B	C	SUM
1	98	54	7	159
2	X = 2	X = −1	X = $\frac{4}{3}$	$\frac{7}{3}$ or $2\frac{1}{3}$
3	$\frac{13}{15}$ = 0.26 = 26%	$\frac{13}{15}$ = 0.26 = 26%	$\frac{24}{50}$ = 0.48 = 48%	1 or 100%
4	Yes, 50	No, 0	Yes, 61	111
5	6	34.56 cm^2	13.82 cm^3	54.38

ABC Sum Race Scorecard

	A	B	C	SUM
1				
2				
3				
4				
5				
6				
7				
8				
9				
10				
11				
12				
13				
14				
15				
16				
17				
18				
19				
20				

Grid Games: Circles

$$C = 2\pi r = \pi d \qquad A = \pi r^2$$

Find the circumference and/or area of each circle with the given radius (r) or diameter (d).

	A	B	C	D	E	F
1	12	r = 3	20	18	r = 4	13
2	r = 2	22	19	r = 7	d = 6	12
3	28	d = 1	d = 9	r = 8	20	d = 12
4	r = 9	22	d = 8	12	d = 14	r = 5
5	d = 16	r = 1	18	14	d = 20	15
6	28	d = 1	40	d = 4	14	15

www.gridgamesgalore.com

Circles Scorecard

	A	B	C	D	E	F
1						
2						
3						
4						
5						
6						

Circles Answer Key

	A	B	C	D	E	F
1	$C = 12\pi$ $A = 36\pi$	$C = 6\pi$ $A = 9\pi$	$C = 40\pi$ $A = 400\pi$	$C = 18\pi$ $A = 81\pi$	$C = 8\pi$ $A = 16\pi$	$C = 26\pi$ $A = 169\pi$
2	$C = 4\pi$ $A = 4\pi$	$C = 44\pi$ $A = 484\pi$	$C = 38\pi$ $A = 361\pi$	$C = 14\pi$ $A = 49\pi$	$C = 6\pi$ $A = 9\pi$	$C = 30\pi$ $A = 225\pi$
3	$C = 56\pi$ $A = 784\pi$	$C = 1\pi$ $A = \frac{1}{4}\pi$	$C = 9\pi$ $A = 8\frac{1}{4}\pi$	$C = 16\pi$ $A = 64\pi$	$C = 20\pi$ $A = 100\pi$	$C = 12\pi$ $A = 36\pi$
4	$C = 18\pi$ $A = 81\pi$	$C = 22\pi$ $A = 121\pi$	$C = 8\pi$ $A = 16\pi$	$C = 24\pi$ $A = 144\pi$	$C = 14\pi$ $A = 49\pi$	$C = 10\pi$ $A = 25\pi$
5	$C = 16\pi$ $A = 64\pi$	$C = 2\pi$ $A = 1\pi$	$C = 36\pi$ $A = 324\pi$	$C = 14\pi$ $A = 49\pi$	$C = 20\pi$ $A = 100\pi$	$C = 30\pi$ $A = 225\pi$
6	$C = 28\pi$ $A = 196\pi$	$C = 1\pi$ $A = \frac{1}{4}\pi$	$C = 40\pi$ $A = 400\pi$	$C = 4\pi$ $A = 4\pi$	$C = 28\pi$ $A = 196\pi$	$C = 15\pi$ $A = 22\frac{5}{4}\pi$

www.gridgamesgalore.com

Grid Games: Squares and Square Roots 2

Solve each story problem involving square roots.

	A	B	C	D	E
1	A square has an area of 25 ft². What is the measure of each side?	√71 falls between which two whole numbers?	√150 falls between which two whole numbers?	A square picture has an area of 169 in². What is the measure of each side?	√50 falls between which two whole numbers?
2	√98 falls between which two whole numbers?	√150 is close to which whole number?	√15 falls between which two whole numbers?	√98 is close to which whole number?	A square has an area of 64 cm². What is the measure of each side?
3	√66 is close to which whole number?	A square has an area of 81 mm². What is the measure of each side?	√47 is close to which whole number?	√55 is close to which whole number?	√200 falls between which two whole numbers?
4	A square sign on the highway has an area of 196 ft². What is the measure of one side?	√70 falls between which two whole numbers?	A square card has an area of 144 cm². What is the measure of each side?	√30 falls between which two whole numbers?	A square poster has an area of 225 cm². What is the measure of each side?
5	√111 falls between which two whole numbers?	√10 is close to which whole number?	√180 falls between which two whole numbers?	A square paper has an area of 49 in². What is the measure of one side?	√40 is close to which whole number?

Squares and Square Roots 2 Scorecard

	A	B	C	D	E
1					
2					
3					
4					
5					

Squares and Square Roots 2 Answer Key

	A	B	C	D	E
1	5 ft	8 and 9	12 and 13	13 in	7 and 8
2	9 and 10	12	3 and 4	10	8 cm
3	8	9 mm	7	7	14 and 15
4	14 ft	8 and 9	12 cm	5 and 6	15 cm
5	10 and 11	3	13 and 14	7 in	6

www.gridgamesgalore.com

Grid Games: Absolute Value

Simplify each expression below.

	A	B	C	D	E	F
1	$\lvert 3 - 2\rvert + 5$ when x = 6	$3\lvert 9 - 38\rvert$	$-2\lvert 51 - 74\rvert$	$\lvert 16 - 21\rvert - 41$	$12 - \lvert x + 10\rvert$ when x = −2	$\lvert 8 - 3x\rvert$ when x = −5
2	$-2\lvert 11 - 28\rvert$	$5 + \lvert x - 14\rvert$ when x = −8	$8 - \lvert 14 - 3x\rvert$ when x = −5	$11 + \lvert x + 6\rvert$ when x = −5	$-\lvert 5 - 19\rvert + 4$	$-\lvert 51 - 39\rvert$
3	$\lvert 5 - 2x\rvert - 5$ when x = 3	$-2\lvert 2 - 27\rvert$	$5 + \lvert 4 - 6x\rvert$ when x = 5	$\frac{1}{2}\lvert 49 - 31\rvert$	$-\frac{1}{2}\lvert 12 + (-34)$	$\lvert 13 - x\rvert + 4$ when x = −4
4	$-2\lvert -14 - 21\rvert$	$7 - \lvert 4x + 9\rvert$ when x = −1	$\lvert 32 - (-23)\rvert$	$12 - \lvert x - 4\rvert$ when x = 8	$\lvert 9 - 3x\rvert - 6$ when x = 4	$\lvert -14 - 37\rvert$
5	$12 - \lvert x - 11\rvert$ when x = 8	$-\frac{1}{3}\lvert -12 + 42\rvert$	$\frac{3}{5}\lvert 8 - 63\rvert$	$\lvert 2x + 3\rvert + 1$ when x = 6	$3 - \lvert x - 4\rvert$ when x = 9	$-3\lvert -7 + (-18)\rvert$
6	$-\lvert 10 - 21\rvert - 8$	$\lvert 5 + 2x\rvert + 11$ when x = −4	$12 - \lvert x - 11\rvert$ when x = 8	$-\frac{1}{2}\lvert 8 - 43$	$\lvert -8 - 12\rvert - 17$	$\lvert 12 - x\rvert - 4$ when x = −7

Absolute Value Scorecard

	A	B	C	D	E	F
1						
2						
3						
4						
5						
6						

Absolute Value Answer Key

	A	B	C	D	E	F
1	21	87	−46	−36	4	23
2	−34	27	−21	12	−10	−12
3	−4	−50	31	9	−11	21
4	−70	2	55	8	−3	51
5	9	−10	33	16	−2	−75
6	−19	14	9	½	3	15

www.gridgamesgalore.com

Matching Mania: Inequalities

h. $2x + 6 \geq -8$	**k.** $2x + 3 < 9$	**f.** $-x - 8 \geq -5$	**i.** $2x - 4 \leq -8$
a. $x + -4 \leq -3$	**m.** $-3x - 4 < 5$	**c.** $-x - 5 \geq 8$	**n.** $-3x \leq 9$
l. $5x < 5$	**b.** $-2x - 15 \leq 3$	**o.** $4x \geq 24$	**d.** $4x - 2 < 0$
j. $-15 \leq -3x$	**g.** $9x + 7 \leq 8x - 2$	**p.** $3x \geq -12$	**e.** $5 > x$

N. $x \leq -9$	**D.** $x \geq -4$	**J.** $x < 5$	**C.** $x \leq 5$
H. $x > -3$	**A.** $x \leq -13$	**I.** $x \geq -9$	**L.** $x \leq 1$
B. $x \geq -3$	**G.** $x \geq 6$	**M.** $x < \dfrac{1}{2}$	**K.** $x < 1$
O. $x < 3$	**F.** $x \leq -3$	**E.** $x \leq -2$	**P.** $x \geq -7$

www.gridgamesgalore.com

Inequalities Scorecard

Graph	Inequality	Solution	Translate to words
1			
2			
3			
4			
5			
6			
7			
8			
9			
10			
11			
12			
13			
14			
15			
16			

Inequalities Answer Key

Graph	Inequality	Solution	Translate to Words
1	f	F	A number less than or equal to −3
2	p	D	A number greater than or equal to −4
3	g	N	A number less than or equal to −9
4	o	G	A number greater than or equal to 6
5	a	L	A number greater than or equal to −9
6	d	M	A number less than or equal to 5
7	j	C	A number less than ½
8	b	I	A number less than or equal to 1
9	e	J	A number less than 5
10	k	O	A number less than 4
11	n	B	A number greater than or equal to −3
12	l	K	A number less than ½
13	m	H	A number greater than −3
14	c	A	A number less than or equal to −13
15	h	P	A number greater than or equal to −7
16	i	E	A number less than or equal to −2

Matching Mania: Integer Operations

1 —11　　9		**2** —10　　14	
3 14　　—5		**4** 9　　—16	
5 21　　—3		**6** —21　　11	
7 —15　　—11		**8** 8　　—20	
9 —10　　24		**10** —17　　—3	
11 —5　　11		**12** —24　　—19	
13 1　　—7		**14** —3　　18	
15 —21　　—15		**16** 0　　—15	
17 —9　　4		**18** —5　　18	

A. **sum = −43**	**R.** **sum = 18**
B. **sum = −36**	**Q.** **sum = 15**
C. **sum = −26**	**P.** **sum = 14**
D. **sum = −20**	**O.** **sum = 13**
E. **sum = −15**	**N.** **sum = 9**
F. **sum = −12**	**M.** **sum = 6**
G. **sum = −10**	**L.** **sum = 4**
H. **sum = −7**	**K.** **sum = −2**
I. **sum = −6**	**J.** **sum = −5**

A. difference = −34	**R.** difference = −32
B. difference = −24	**Q.** difference = −23
C. difference = −21	**P.** difference = −20
D. difference = −16	**O.** difference = −14
E. difference = −13	**N.** difference = −6
F. difference = −5	**M.** difference = −4
G. difference = 8	**L.** difference = 15
H. difference = 19	**K.** difference = 24
I. difference = 25	**J.** difference = 28

a. product = 456	r. product = 315
b. product = 165	q. product = 51
c. product = 0	p. product = −7
d. product = −36	o. product = −54
e. product = −55	n. product = −63
f. product = −70	m. product = −90
g. product = −99	l. product = −140
h. product = −144	k. product = −160
i. product = −231	j. product = −240

Integer Operations Scorecards

Integers	Sum	Difference	Product
1			
2			
3			
4			
5			
6			
7			
8			
9			
10			
11			
12			
13			
14			
15			
16			
17			
18			

Integers	Sum	Difference	Product
1			
2			
3			
4			
5			
6			
7			
8			
9			
10			
11			
12			
13			
14			
15			
16			
17			
18			

Integer Operations Answer Key

Integers	Sum	Difference	Product
1	K	P	g
2	L	B	l
3	N	H	f
4	H	I	h
5	R	K	n
6	G	R	i
7	C	M	b
8	F	J	k
9	P	A	j
10	D	O	q
11	M	D	e
12	A	F	a
13	I	G	p
14	Q	C	o
15	B	N	r
16	E	L	c
17	J	E	d
18	O	Q	m

www.gridgamesgalore.com

Matching Mania: Linear Functions

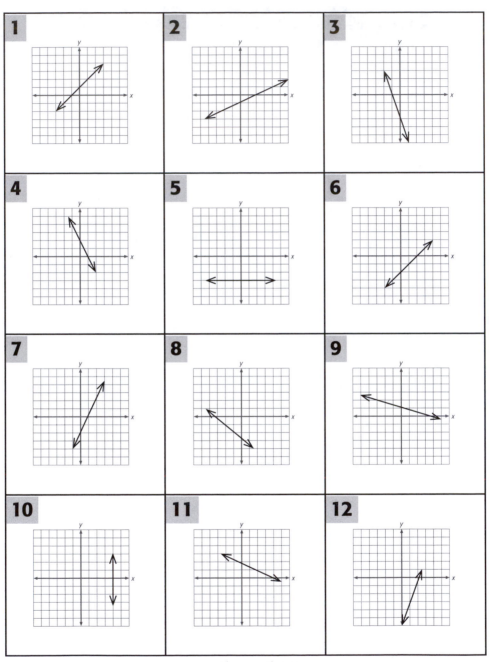

A. $y = -3x - 3$	**B.** $y = -2x + 2$
C. $y = \frac{1}{2}x - 1$	**D.** $y = 2x - 2$
E. $x = 4$	**F.** $y = x + 1$
G. $y = \frac{1}{2}x + 2$	**H.** $y = -x - 3$
I. $y = -\frac{1}{3} + 1$	**J.** $y = -3$
K. $y = x - 2$	**L.** $y = 3x - 6$

a. $$m = -2$$ $$b = 2$$	**b.** $$m = 2$$ $$b = -2$$
c. $$m = \frac{1}{2}$$ $$b = 2$$	**d.** $$m = 1$$ $$b = 1$$
e. $$m = -1$$ $$b = -3$$	**f.** $$m = 0$$ $$b = -3$$
g. $$m = \frac{1}{2}$$ $$b = -1$$	**h.** $$m = \frac{1}{3}$$ $$b = 1$$
i. $$m = 1$$ $$b = -2$$	**j.** $$m = -3$$ $$b = -3$$
k. $$m = 3$$ $$b = -6$$	**l.** **m is undefined** **no b value**

Linear Functions Scorecards

Graph	Slope Intercept Form	Slope and y-intercept
1		
2		
3		
4		
5		
6		
7		
8		
9		
10		
11		
12		

Graph	Slope Intercept Form	Slope and y-intercept
1		
2		
3		
4		
5		
6		
7		
8		
9		
10		
11		
12		

Linear Functions Answer Key

Graph	Slope-Intercept Form	Slope and y-intercept
1	F	d
2	C	g
3	A	j
4	B	a
5	J	f
6	K	i
7	D	b
8	H	e
9	I	h
10	E	l
11	G	c
12	L	k

Walk This Way: Linear Equations

Assigned *x*-coordinate _____

Solve the following equations for *y* and then write as an ordered pair:

y = x   **Ordered pair (_____ , _____) (Parent Function)**
y = −x   Ordered pair (_____ , _____)
y = x + 3   Ordered pair (_____ , _____)
y = x − 3   Ordered pair (_____ , _____)
y = 3x   Ordered pair (_____ , _____)
$y = \frac{1}{3}x$ Ordered pair (_____ , _____)

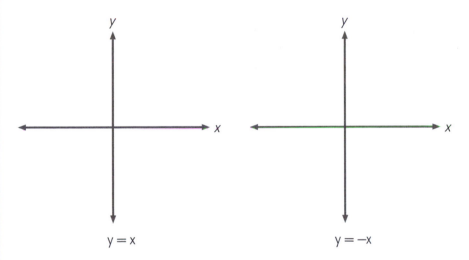

y = x   y = −x

Compare the graph of y = x and y = −x. What do you notice about the difference in the look of the two graphs? Discuss what component in the equation is responsible for the observed transformation.

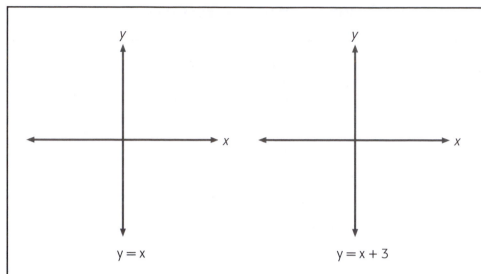

y = x   y = x + 3

Compare the graph of y = x and y = x + 3. What do you notice about the difference in the look of the two graphs? Discuss what component in the equation is responsible for the observed transformation.

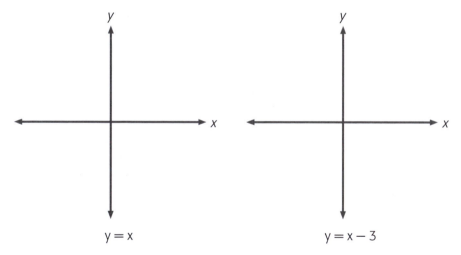

y = x   y = x − 3

Compare the graph of y = x and y = x − 3. What do you notice about the difference in the look of the two graphs? Discuss what component in the equation is responsible for the observed transformation.

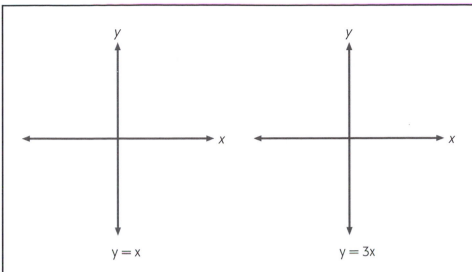

Compare the graph of y = x and y = 3x. What do you notice about the difference in the look of the two graphs? Discuss what component in the equation is responsible for the observed transformation.

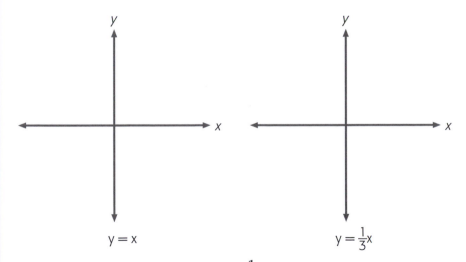

Compare the graph of y = x and y = $\frac{1}{3}$x. What do you notice about the difference in the look of the two graphs? Discuss what component in the equation is responsible for the observed transformation.

What do you think the graph of y = −3x + 1 will look like? Explain your reasoning.

Appendix B

Standards for Mathematical Practice*

————◼————

The Standards for Mathematical Practice describe varieties of expertise that mathematics educators at all levels should seek to develop in their students. These practices rest on important "processes and proficiencies" with longstanding importance in mathematics education. The first of these are the NCTM process standards of problem solving, reasoning and proof, communication, representation, and connections. The second are the strands of mathematical proficiency specified in the National Research Council's report *Adding It Up*: adaptive reasoning, strategic competence, conceptual understanding (comprehension of mathematical concepts, operations and relations), procedural fluency (skill in carrying out procedures flexibly, accurately, efficiently and appropriately), and productive disposition (habitual inclination to see mathematics as sensible, useful, and worthwhile, coupled with a belief in diligence and one's own efficacy).

1 Make sense of problems and persevere in solving them.

Mathematically proficient students start by explaining to themselves the meaning of a problem and looking for entry points to its solution. They analyze givens, constraints, relationships, and goals. They make conjectures about the form and meaning of the solution and plan a solution pathway rather than simply jumping into a solution attempt. They consider analogous problems, and try special cases and simpler forms of the original problem in order to gain insight into its solution. They monitor and evaluate their progress and change course if necessary. Older students might, depending on the context of the problem, transform algebraic expressions or change the viewing window on their graphing calculator to get the information they need. Mathematically proficient students can explain correspondences between equations, verbal descriptions, tables, and graphs or draw diagrams of important features and relationships, graph data, and search for regularity or trends. Younger students might rely on using

*Common Core State Standards Initiative. (2012). Standards for Mathematical Practice (pp. 6–8). Retrieved from http://www.corestandards.org/assets/CCSSI_Math%20Standards.pdf

concrete objects or pictures to help conceptualize and solve a problem. Mathematically proficient students check their answers to problems using a different method, and they continually ask themselves, "Does this make sense?" They can understand the approaches of others to solving complex problems and identify correspondences between different approaches.

2   Reason abstractly and quantitatively.

Mathematically proficient students make sense of quantities and their relationships in problem situations. They bring two complementary abilities to bear on problems involving quantitative relationships: the ability to *decontextualize*—to abstract a given situation and represent it symbolically and manipulate the representing symbols as if they have a life of their own, without necessarily attending to their referents—and the ability to *contextualize*, to pause as needed during the manipulation process in order to probe into the referents for the symbols involved. Quantitative reasoning entails habits of creating a coherent representation of the problem at hand; considering the units involved; attending to the meaning of quantities, not just how to compute them; and knowing and flexibly using different properties of operations and objects.

3   Construct viable arguments and critique the reasoning of others.

Mathematically proficient students understand and use stated assumptions, definitions, and previously established results in constructing arguments. They make conjectures and build a logical progression of statements to explore the truth of their conjectures. They are able to analyze situations by breaking them into cases, and can recognize and use counterexamples. They justify their conclusions, communicate them to others, and respond to the arguments of others. They reason inductively about data, making plausible arguments that take into account the context from which the data arose. Mathematically proficient students are also able to compare the effectiveness of two plausible arguments, distinguish correct logic or reasoning from that which is flawed, and—if there is a flaw in an argument—explain what it is. Elementary students can construct arguments using concrete referents such as objects, drawings, diagrams, and actions. Such arguments can make sense and be correct, even though they are not generalized or made formal until later grades. Later, students learn to determine domains to which an argument applies. Students at all grades can listen or read the arguments of others, decide whether they make sense, and ask useful questions to clarify or improve the arguments.

4   Model with mathematics.

Mathematically proficient students can apply the mathematics they know to solve problems arising in everyday life, society, and the workplace.

In early grades, this might be as simple as writing an addition equation to describe a situation. In middle grades, a student might apply proportional reasoning to plan a school event or analyze a problem in the community. By high school, a student might use geometry to solve a design problem or use a function to describe how one quantity of interest depends on another. Mathematically proficient students who can apply what they know are comfortable making assumptions and approximations to simplify a complicated situation, realizing that these may need revision later. They are able to identify important quantities in a practical situation and map their relationships using such tools as diagrams, two-way tables, graphs, flowcharts and formulas. They can analyze those relationships mathematically to draw conclusions. They routinely interpret their mathematical results in the context of the situation and reflect on whether the results make sense, possibly improving the model if it has not served its purpose.

5 Use appropriate tools strategically.

Mathematically proficient students consider the available tools when solving a mathematical problem. These tools might include pencil and paper, concrete models, a ruler, a protractor, a calculator, a spreadsheet, a computer algebra system, a statistical package, or dynamic geometry software. Proficient students are sufficiently familiar with tools appropriate for their grade or course to make sound decisions about when each of these tools might be helpful, recognizing both the insight to be gained and their limitations. For example, mathematically proficient high school students analyze graphs of functions and solutions generated using a graphing calculator. They detect possible errors by strategically using estimation and other mathematical knowledge. When making mathematical models, they know that technology can enable them to visualize the results of varying assumptions, explore consequences, and compare predictions with data. Mathematically proficient students at various grade levels are able to identify relevant external mathematical resources, such as digital content located on a website, and use them to pose or solve problems. They are able to use technological tools to explore and deepen their understanding of concepts.

6 Attend to precision.

Mathematically proficient students try to communicate precisely to others. They try to use clear definitions in discussion with others and in their own reasoning. They state the meaning of the symbols they choose, including using the equal sign consistently and appropriately. They are careful about specifying units of measure, and labeling axes to clarify the correspondence with quantities in a problem. They calculate accurately and efficiently, express numerical answers with a degree of precision appropriate for the problem context. In the elementary grades, students give carefully formulated explanations to each other. By the time they reach high school they have learned to examine claims and make explicit use of definitions.

7   Look for and make use of structure.

Mathematically proficient students look closely to discern a pattern or structure. Young students, for example, might notice that three and seven more is the same amount as seven and three more, or they may sort a collection of shapes according to how many sides the shapes have. Later, students will see 7×8 equals the well remembered $7 \times 5 + 7 \times 3$, in preparation for learning about the distributive property. In the expression $x^2 + 9x + 14$, older students can see the 14 as 2×7 and the 9 as $2 + 7$. They recognize the significance of an existing line in a geometric figure and can use the strategy of drawing an auxiliary line for solving problems. They also can step back for an overview and shift perspective. They can see complicated things, such as some algebraic expressions, as single objects or as being composed of several objects. For example, they can see $5 - 3(x - y)^2$ as 5 minus a positive number times a square and use that to realize that its value cannot be more than 5 for any real numbers x and y.

8 Look for and express regularity in repeated reasoning.

Mathematically proficient students notice if calculations are repeated, and look both for general methods and for shortcuts. Upper elementary students might notice when dividing 25 by 11 that they are repeating the same calculations over and over again, and conclude they have a repeating decimal. By paying attention to the calculation of slope as they repeatedly check whether points are on the line through (1, 2) with slope 3, middle school students might abstract the equation $(y - 2)/(x - 1) = 3$. Noticing the regularity in the way terms cancel when expanding $(x - 1)(x + 1)$, $(x - 1)(x^2 + x + 1)$, and $(x - 1)(x^3 + x^2 + x + 1)$ might lead them to the general formula for the sum of a geometric series. As they work to solve a problem, mathematically proficient students maintain oversight of the process, while attending to the details. They continually evaluate the reasonableness of their intermediate results.

Connecting the Standards for Mathematical Practice to the Standards for Mathematical Content

The Standards for Mathematical Practice describe ways in which developing student practitioners of the discipline of mathematics increasingly ought to engage with the subject matter as they grow in mathematical maturity and expertise throughout the elementary, middle and high school years. Designers of curricula, assessments, and professional development should all attend to the need to connect the mathematical practices to mathematical content in mathematics instruction.

The Standards for Mathematical Content are a balanced combination of procedure and understanding. Expectations that begin with the word "understand" are often especially good opportunities to connect the practices to the content. Students who lack understanding of a topic may rely on procedures too heavily. Without a flexible base from which to work, they may be less likely to consider analogous problems, represent problems coherently, justify conclusions, apply the mathematics to practical situations, use technology mindfully to work with the mathematics, explain the mathematics accurately to other students, step back for an overview, or deviate from a known procedure to find a shortcut. In short, a lack of understanding effectively prevents a student from engaging in the mathematical practices.

In this respect, those content standards which set an expectation of understanding are potential "points of intersection" between the Standards for Mathematical Content and the Standards for Mathematical Practice. These points of intersection are intended to be weighted toward central and generative concepts in the school mathematics curriculum that most merit the time, resources, innovative energies, and focus necessary to qualitatively improve the curriculum, instruction, assessment, professional development, and student achievement in mathematics.

Common Core State Standards for Mathematics 6–8 Nomenclature Key

Grade Level Identifiers	
Sixth Grade	6
Seventh Grade	7
Eighth Grade	8

Domain Identifiers		
Ratios & Proportional Relationships	RP	Grades 6, 7, 8
The Number System	NS	Grades 6, 7, 8
Expressions & Equations	EE	Grades 6, 7, 8
Statistics & Probability	SP	Grades 6*, 7, 8*
Functions	F	Grade 8

*Probability only occurs in Seventh Grade

CCSS.Math.Content.8.F.A.3 is interpreted as the third standard in the first cluster in the Function domain in the eighth-grade standards.

Standards Alignment—Middle School

The strategies can be used with any content standard. The list below simply references the ones used as examples.

	Ratios and Proportional Relationships (6th/7th) Functions (8th)	The Number System	Expressions and Equations	Geometry	Statistics and Probability
Problem-Solving Process				6.G.A.2 7.G.B.4 7.G.B.6 8.G.C.9	
Visual Vocabulary	6.RP.A.1 6.RP.A.2 7.RP.A.2			6.G.A.2 7.G.B.4 7.G.B.6 8.G.C.9	
Puzzling Problems				7.G.B.4	6.SP.A.2 6.SP.A.3 6.SP.B.5 6.SP.B.5c 6.SP.B.5d 7.SP.C.5 7.SP.C.6 8.SP.A.1 8.SP.A.2 8.SP.A.3

	Ratios and Proportional Relationships (6th/7th) Functions (8th)	The Number System	Expressions and Equations	Geometry	Statistics and Probability
ABC Sum Race			6.EE.A.1 6.EE.A.2 6.EE.A.2a 6.EE.A.2b 6.EE.A.2c 6.EE.B.5 7.EE.A.1 8.EE.A.1 8.EE.C.7 8.EE.C.7a 8.EE.C.7b	6.G.A.2 6.G.A.4 7.G.B.6 8.G.B.7	7.SP.C.8 7.SP.C.8a 7.SP.C.8b 7.SP.C.8c
Grid Games		6.NS.C.7 6.NS.C.7c	8.EE.A.2	7.G.B.4	
Matching Mania	8.F.A.3	6.NS.C.5 7.NS.A.1	6.EE.B.5 6.EE.B.8 7.EE.B.4 7.EE.B.4b		